VB.NET

CROSSING OVER

VB.Net Does VBScript

Richard Thomas Edwards

CONTENTS

And why not
The Scriptomatic paved the way

Years ago, some creative scripting authors came up with a relatively simple tool called the Scriptomatic. It was so popular that two versions of it were developed and several spinoffs were created.

Unfortunately, the Scriptomatic never really did all the things it was supposed to do. Some options didn't work, additional language support wasn't completed and the classes WMI supported were not completely documented.

Despite these flaws, the concept of a single resource that did many things with few options and lots of effect was born. And the word PowerShell was breathed into a one size fits all Sherman tank or a product.

On the other side of that development process, I was creating programs that write programs – yes, PWPSquared.Net and PWPSquared.Com were both my websites back in the early 2000's – and I was discovering that the parent\child relationship between writing a resource wrapper around the languages I was familiar with, could, indeed, be used to write other programming languages I was not so familiar with.

There were additional benefits when writing code this way.

Once the basic code was written and tested, only a couple of minor tweaks in the code could turn the code into something else completely different and for a completely different purpose.

The squared part of the domain name came about when I and another programmer friend of mine, Warren Halcott, were able to write a VBScript that generated an output from within the code itself.

Here's an example of how that worked.

```
Set ws = createobject("WScript.Shell")
Set fso = CreateObject("Scripting.FileSystemObject")
Set txtstream = fso.OpenTextFile(ws.CurrentDirectory & "\Services.xml", 2, true,
-2)
```

The code would then write the xml data file and then the code would write the HTML file that would have the "<XML ID=""rs"" src=""" & ws.CurrentDirectory & "\Services.xml""/>"

Now, that, combined with VB6 or VB.Net as the parent, wrote out the code and was the other part of the Program that writes programs...squared. Of course, what is known as a heavy client went away.

Or, so we thought. Fact is, both the IDE and the HTA Browser environment for Visual Studio 2017 and shipped with Windows Server 2016 still support these kinds of programs. But, of course, that isn't true with the commercial version of the Web Browser.

But we weren't limited to the Web Browser anyway as we could write programs that used Office products and just about any other product that we could use to get the job done.

Going Multi-Language Code Surfing

Please feel free to surf the web for examples you want to use other than the ones I'm using. I don't pretend that I am an expert in all the languages that supports COM and NET languages. But I do know almost 20 to know that each one of those languages can easily be produced using VB6 and VB.Net. And since I write a lot of code using Active Directory Services, database and WMI code, I also know that an entire book on the each one. So, if you have gotten to here and you purchase another book, this is where your journey through that book actually begins.

If there is a language that works for you and you have the code that can be automated, you should be able to use VB.Net to produce the front-end interface and automate the development cycle.

Inside this book, I'm going to be using VBScript as the output coding engine and working with ADO, DAO, and WMI to produce reports.

Let's get started.

Designing the front end
Using the KISS Principle

The first thing I want to cover is concept of KISS or keep it simple, stupid approach. Since our first front end involves ADO, there are two things you must have to make the code work:

- A connection string
- A Query string

When you have both of those and you know they are working, your next step is to decide on what combination of Connection, Command and Recordset you want to use. And honestly, the Recordset can stand on its own two feet.

Connection, Command And Recordset

```
Set cn = CreateObject("Adodb.Connection")
Set cmd = CreateObject("Adodb.Command")
Set rs = CreateObject("Adodb.Recordset")

cn.ConnectionString = cnstr
Call cn.Open()

cmd.ActiveConnection = cn
cmd.CommandType = 1
cmd.CommandText = strQuery
```

```
rs = cmd.Execute()
```

Okay so, what is this used for? This code example is used to produce a forward only recordset. It is fast. But you can't use it for adding additional rows or perform edits and updates.

If you want a more robust coding scenario, you'll want to use the connection and Recordset combination or just the recordset. However, the combination of all three can produce a RecordCount which can be used for adding records and editing and updating columns.

```
Set cn = CreateObject("Adodb.Connection")
cmd = CreateObject("Adodb.Command")
Set rs = CreateObject("Adodb.Recordset")

cn.ConnectionString = cnstr
Call cn.Open()

cmd.ActiveConnection = cn
cmd.CommandType = 1
cmd.CommandText = strQuery
cmd.Execute()

rs.ActiveConnection = cn
rs.Cursorlocation = 3
rs.Locktype = 3
Call rs.Open(cmd)
```

Now, you can get the RecordCount and do AddNew, edit, delete and updates on the table.

Connection And Recordset

```
cn = CreateObject("Adodb.Connection")
Set rs = CreateObject("Adodb.Recordset")
Cn.ConnectionString = cnstr
Cn.Open()

Rs.ActiveConnection = cn
rs.Cursorlocation = 3
rs.Locktype = 3
rs.Source = strQuery
rs.Open()
```

Again, you can get the RecordCount and do AddNew, edit, delete and updates on the table

Command And Recordset

```
Set cmd = CreateObject("Adodb.Command")
Set rs = CreateObject("Adodb.Recordset")
cmd.ActiveConnection = cnstr
cmd.CommandType = 1
cmd.CommandText = strQuery
rs = cmd.Execute()
Or
Call cmd.Execute()
rs.Cursorlocation = 3
rs.Locktype = 3
rs.Open(cmd)
```

Now, you can get the RecordCount and do AddNew, edit, delete and updates on the table.

Recordset

```
Set rs = CreateObject("Adodb.Recordset")
rs.ActiveConnection = cnstr
rs.Cursorlocation = 3
rs.Locktype = 3
rs.Source = strQuery
rs.Open()
```

Of course, these lines wouldn't be written this way. There would be a select case statement followed by what you selected:

```
txtstream.WriteLine("cnstr = ""Provider=Microsoft.Jet.OleDb.4.0;Data Source
=C:\Program Files (x96)\Microsoft Visual Studio\VB98\nwind.mdb;"" ")
txtstream.WriteLine("strQuery = ""Select * From Products"" ")

Select Case ComboBox1.Text

    Case "Connection, Command and Recordset

    txtstream.WriteLine("Set cn = CreateObject(""Adodb.Connection"")")
    txtstream.WriteLine("cn.ConnectionString = cnstr")
    txtstream.WriteLine("Call cn.Open()")
    txtstream.WriteLine("")
    txtstream.WriteLine("Set cmd = CreateObject(""Adodb.Command"")")
    txtstream.WriteLine("cmd.ActiveConnection = cn")
    txtstream.WriteLine("cmd.CommandType = 1")
    txtstream.WriteLine("cmd.CommandText = strQuery")
```

```
txtstream.WriteLine("Call cmd.Execute()")
txtstream.WriteLine("")
txtstream.WriteLine("Set rs = CreateObject(""Adodb.Recordset"")")
txtstream.WriteLine("rs.Cursorlocation = 3")
txtstream.WriteLine("rs.Locktype = 3")
txtstream.WriteLine("rs.Open(cmd)")


Case "Connection And Recordset


txtstream.WriteLine("Set cn = CreateObject(""Adodb.Connection"")")
txtstream.WriteLine("cn.ConnectionString = cnstr")
txtstream.WriteLine("Call cn.Open()")
txtstream.WriteLine("")
txtstream.WriteLine("Set rs = CreateObject(""Adodb.Recordset"")")
txtstream.WriteLine("rs.Cursorlocation = 3")
txtstream.WriteLine("rs.Locktype = 3")
txtstream.WriteLine("rs.Open(strQuery, cn)")



Case "Command And Recordset


txtstream.WriteLine("Set cmd = CreateObject(""Adodb.Command"")")
txtstream.WriteLine("Set rs = CreateObject(""Adodb.Recordset"")")
txtstream.WriteLine("cmd.ActiveConnection = cnstr")
txtstream.WriteLine("cmd.CommandType = 1")
txtstream.WriteLine("cmd.CommandText = strQuery")
txtstream.WriteLine("Call cmd.Execute()")
txtstream.WriteLine("rs.Cursorlocation = 3")
txtstream.WriteLine("rs.Locktype = 3")
txtstream.WriteLine("rs.Open(cmd)")



Case "Recordset"


txtstream.WriteLine("Set rs = CreateObject(""Adodb.Recordset"")")
txtstream.WriteLine("rs.ActiveConnection = cnstr")
txtstream.WriteLine("rs.Cursorlocation = 3")
txtstream.WriteLine("rs.Locktype = 3")
```

```
txtstream.WriteLine("rs.Source = strQuery")
txtstream.WriteLine("rs.Open")
```

End Select

Of course, you could get as sophisticated as you desire with combo boxes used for CursorType, CursorLocation, LockType, and so forth and so on. You can even use the connection object to list all of the different Tables and Views that are inside the database.

You can also refine your queries with a `CheckedListBox` where you return only those Items you've chosen:

Whatever way you do it, the bottom line is when you click the create the code button, all of what you've selected along with how you want to render the information. I generally have a suite of possible outputs that looks like this:

- ⊟ **ASP**
  - ⊞ Reports
  - ⊞ Tables
- ⊟ ASPX
  - ⊞ Reports
  - ⊞ Tables
- Attribute XML
- ⊟ Colon Delimited File
  - Horizontal
  - Vertical
- ⊟ CSV File
  - Horizontal
  - Vertical
- Element XML
- Element XML For XSL
- ⊟ Exclamation Delimited File
  - Horizontal
  - Vertical
- ⊟ Excel using a CSV File
  - Horizontal
  - Vertical
- ⊟ Excel Automation
  - Horizontal
  - Vertical
- Excel Spreadsheet
- ⊟ HTA
  - ⊞ Reports
  - ⊞ Tables
- ⊟ HTML
  - ⊞ Reports
  - ⊞ Tables
- Schema XML
- ⊟ Semi-Colon Delimited File
  - Horizontal
  - Vertical
- ⊟ Tab Delimited File
  - Horizontal
  - Vertical
- ⊟ XSL
  - ⊞ Reports
  - ⊞ Tables

And the Module looks like this:

```
Public cnstr As String
Public strQuery As String
Public EngineType As String
Public Tablename As String
Public OutputType As String
Public Orientation As String
Public ControlType As String
Public TableType As String
Public txtstream As Object
Public fso As Object = CreateObject("Scripting.FileSystemObject")
Public Stylesheet As String


Public Sub Start_The_Show()

    Dim txtatream As Object = fso.OpenTextFile(Application.StartupPath & "\" &
Tablename & ".txt", 2, True, -2)

    txtstream.WriteLine("")
    txtstream.WriteLine("cnstr = ""Provider=Microsoft.Jet.OleDb.4.0;Data Source
=C:\Program Files (x96)\Microsoft Visual Studio\VB98\nwind.mdb;"" ")
    txtstream.WriteLine("strQuery = ""Select * From Products"" ")
    txtstream.WriteLine("")


End Sub


Public Sub Write_The_Code(ByVal OutputType As String)


    Start_The_VBScript_Code()

    Select Case OutputType

      Case "Attribute XML"

          Do_Attribute_XML_Code()

      Case "Element XML"

          Do_Element_XML_Code()

      Case "Element XML For XSL"

          Do_Element_XML_For_XSL_Code()
```

```vbscript
        Case "Schema XML"

            Do_Schema_XML_Code()

    End Select

    End_All_Others()


End Sub

Public Sub Write_The_Code1(ByVal OutputType As String)

    Start_The_VBScript_Code()

    Select Case OutputType

        Case "Colon Delimited File"

            Do_Colon_Delimited_Code()

        Case "CSV File"

            Do_CSV_Code()

        Case "Exclamation Delimited File"

            Do_Exclamation_Delimited_Code()

        Case "Semi-Colon Delimited File"

            Do_Semi_Colon_Delimited_Code()

        Case "Tab Delimited File"

            Do_Tab_Delimited_Code()

        Case "Tilde Delimited File"

            Do_Tilde_Delimited_Code()

    End Select

    End_All_Others()


End Sub

Public Sub Write_The_Code2(ByVal OutputType As String)
```

```vb
        Start_The_VBScript_Code()

    Select Case OutputType

        Case "ASP"

            Write_The_ASP_Code()
            Write_The_ASP_Enumerator_Code()
            End_The_ASP_Code()

        Case "ASPX"

            Write_The_ASPX_Code()
            Write_The_ASP_Enumerator_Code()
            End_The_ASPX_Code()

        Case "HTA"

            Write_The_HTA_Code()
            Write_The_HTML_Enumerator_Code()
            End_The_HTA_Code()

        Case "HTML"

            Write_The_HTML_Code()
            Write_The_HTML_Enumerator_Code()
            End_The_HTML_Code()

        Case "XSL"

            Write_The_XSL_Code()
            End_The_XSL_Code()

    End Select


End Sub


Private Sub Start_The_VBScript_Code()


    txtstream = fso.OpenTextFile(Application.StartupPath & "\" & Tablename &
".vbs", 2, True, -2)


    Select Case EngineType
```

Case "Connection, Command and Recordset"

```vb
        txtstream.WriteLine("    Set cn = CreateObject(""ADODB.Connection"")")
        txtstream.WriteLine("    Set cmd = CreateObject(""ADODB.Command"")")
        txtstream.WriteLine("    Set rs = CreateObject(""ADODB.Recordset"")")
        txtstream.WriteLine("")
        txtstream.WriteLine("    cn.ConnectionString = cnstr")
        txtstream.WriteLine("    Call cn.Open()")
        txtstream.WriteLine("")
        txtstream.WriteLine("    cmd.ActiveConnection = cn")
        txtstream.WriteLine("    cmd.CommandType=1")
        txtstream.WriteLine("    cmd.CommandText = strQuery")
        txtstream.WriteLine("    Call cmd.Execute()")
        txtstream.WriteLine("")
        txtstream.WriteLine("    rs.CursorLocation = 3")
        txtstream.WriteLine("    rs.LockType = 3")
        txtstream.WriteLine("    Call rs.Open(cmd)")
        txtstream.WriteLine("")
        txtstream.WriteLine("    rs.MoveFirst()")
        txtstream.WriteLine("")
```

Case "Connection and Recordset"

```vb
        txtstream.WriteLine("    Set cn = CreateObject(""ADODB.Connection"")")
        txtstream.WriteLine("    Set rs = CreateObject(""ADODB.Recordset"")")
        txtstream.WriteLine("")
        txtstream.WriteLine("    cn.ConnectionString = """" & cnstr & """" ")
        txtstream.WriteLine("    Call cn.Open()")
        txtstream.WriteLine("")
        txtstream.WriteLine("    rs.ActiveConnection = cn")
        txtstream.WriteLine("    rs.CursorLocation = 3")
        txtstream.WriteLine("    rs.LockType = 3")
        txtstream.WriteLine("    Call rs.Open("""" & strQuery & """")")
        txtstream.WriteLine("")
        txtstream.WriteLine("    rs.MoveFirst()")
        txtstream.WriteLine("")
```

Case "Command and Recordset"

```vb
        txtstream.WriteLine("    Set cmd = CreateObject(""ADODB.Command"")")
```

```vb
        txtstream.WriteLine("    Set rs = CreateObject(""ADODB.Recordset"")")
        txtstream.WriteLine("")
        txtstream.WriteLine("    cmd.ActiveConnection = """ & cnstr & """ ")
        txtstream.WriteLine("    cmd.CommandType=1")
        txtstream.WriteLine("    cmd.CommandText = """ & strQuery & """ ")
        txtstream.WriteLine("    Call cmd.Execute()")
        txtstream.WriteLine("")
        txtstream.WriteLine("    rs.CursorLocation = 3")
        txtstream.WriteLine("    rs.LockType = 3")
        txtstream.WriteLine("    Call rs.Open(cmd)")
        txtstream.WriteLine("")
        txtstream.WriteLine("    rs.MoveFirst()")
        txtstream.WriteLine("")


    Case "Recordset"

        txtstream.WriteLine("    Set rs = CreateObject(""ADODB.Recordset"")")
        txtstream.WriteLine("    rs.ActiveConnection = """ & cnstr & """ ")
        txtstream.WriteLine("    rs.CursorLocation = 3")
        txtstream.WriteLine("    rs.LockType = 3")
        txtstream.WriteLine("    rs.Open(""" & strQuery & """)")
        txtstream.WriteLine("")
        txtstream.WriteLine("    rs.MoveFirst()")
        txtstream.WriteLine("")


    End Select


End Sub
```

The ASP, ASPX, HTA And HTML Toppers Code

The next four routines are used to initial the top part of the ASP. ASPX, HTA, and HTML Code.

```
Private Sub Write_The_ASP_Code()


     txtstream.WriteLine("    Set ws = CreateObject(""""WScript.Shell"""")")
     txtstream.WriteLine("    Set fso =
CreateObject(""""Scripting.FileSystemObject"""")")
     txtstream.WriteLine("    Set txtstream = fso.OpenTextFile(ws.CurrentDirectory +
""""\" & Tablename & ".asp"""", 2, True, -2)")
     txtstream.WriteLine("    txtstream.WriteLine(""""<hmtl>"""")")
     txtstream.WriteLine("    txtstream.WriteLine(""""<head>"""")")
     txtstream.WriteLine("    txtstream.WriteLine(""""<title>"""" & Tablename &
""""</title>"""")")
     Add_StyleSheet()
     txtstream.WriteLine("    txtstream.WriteLine(""""<body>"""")")
     txtstream.WriteLine("    txtstream.WriteLine(""""<center>"""")")
     txtstream.WriteLine("    txtstream.WriteLine(""""</br>"""")")
     txtstream.WriteLine("    txtstream.WriteLine(""""<h1 nowrap='nowrap'
STYLE=""""""""background-color:white;FONT-WEIGHT:normal; FONT-SIZE: 48px;
COLOR: navy; FONT-STYLE: normal; FONT-FAMILY: Edwardian Script
ITC"""""""">PlanetMPs  </H1>"""")")
     txtstream.WriteLine("    txtstream.WriteLine(""""</br>"""")")


     Select Case TableType

         Case "Reports"
```

```
        txtstream.WriteLine("    txtstream.WriteLine(""""<table border=0
cellspacing=3 cellpadding=3>"""")")

        Case "Tables"

            txtstream.WriteLine("    txtstream.WriteLine(""""<table
style='border:Double;border-width:1px;border-color:navy;' rules=all frames=both
cellpadding=2 cellspacing=2 Width=0>"""")")

      End Select

      txtstream.WriteLine("    txtstream.WriteLine(""""<%"""")")


   End Sub


   Private Sub Write_The_ASPX_Code()


      txtstream.WriteLine("    Set ws = CreateObject("""WScript.Shell""")")
      txtstream.WriteLine("    Set fso =
CreateObject("""Scripting.FileSystemObject""")")
      txtstream.WriteLine("    Set txtstream = fso.OpenTextFile(ws.CurrentDirectory +
""\" & Tablename & ".aspx""", 2, True, -2)")
      txtstream.WriteLine("    txtstream.WriteLine(""""<hmtl>"""")")
      txtstream.WriteLine("    txtstream.WriteLine(""""<head>"""")")
      txtstream.WriteLine("    txtstream.WriteLine(""""<title>"" & Tablename &
""</title>"""")")
      Add_StyleSheet()
      txtstream.WriteLine("    txtstream.WriteLine(""""<body>"""")")
      txtstream.WriteLine("    txtstream.WriteLine(""""<center>"""")")
      txtstream.WriteLine("    txtstream.WriteLine(""""</br>"""")")
      txtstream.WriteLine("    txtstream.WriteLine(""""<h1 nowrap='nowrap'
STYLE="""""""background-color:white;FONT-WEIGHT:normal; FONT-SIZE: 48px;
COLOR: navy; FONT-STYLE: normal; FONT-FAMILY: Edwardian Script
ITC"""""">PlanetMPs  </H1>"""")")
      txtstream.WriteLine("    txtstream.WriteLine(""""</br>"""")")


      Select Case TableType

        Case "Reports"

            txtstream.WriteLine("    txtstream.WriteLine(""""<table border=0
cellspacing=3 cellpadding=3>"""")")

        Case "Tables"
```

```
        txtstream.WriteLine("    txtstream.WriteLine("""<table
style='border:Double;border-width:1px;border-color:navy;' rules=all frames=both
cellpadding=2 cellspacing=2 Width=0>""")")

    End Select

End Sub

Private Sub Write_The_HTA_Code()


        txtstream.WriteLine("    Set ws = CreateObject(""WScript.Shell"")")
        txtstream.WriteLine("    Set fso =
CreateObject(""Scripting.FileSystemObject"")")
        txtstream.WriteLine("    Set txtstream = fso.OpenTextFile(ws.CurrentDirectory +
""\" & Tablename & ".hta""", 2, True, -2)")
        txtstream.WriteLine("    txtstream.WriteLine(""<hmtl>"")")
        txtstream.WriteLine("    txtstream.WriteLine(""<head>"")")
        txtstream.WriteLine("    txtstream.WriteLine(""<HTA:APPLICATION "")")
        txtstream.WriteLine("    txtstream.WriteLine(""ID = """"""Products"""""" "")")
        txtstream.WriteLine("    txtstream.WriteLine(""APPLICATIONNAME =
""""""Products"""""" "")")
        txtstream.WriteLine("    txtstream.WriteLine(""SCROLL = """"""yes"""""" "")")
        txtstream.WriteLine("    txtstream.WriteLine(""SINGLEINSTANCE =
""""""yes"""""" "")")
        txtstream.WriteLine("    txtstream.WriteLine(""WINDOWSTATE =
""""""maximize"""""" >"")")
        txtstream.WriteLine("    txtstream.WriteLine(""<title>"" & Tablename &
""</title>"")")
        Add_StyleSheet()
        txtstream.WriteLine("    txtstream.WriteLine(""<body>"")")
        txtstream.WriteLine("    txtstream.WriteLine(""<center>"")")
        txtstream.WriteLine("    txtstream.WriteLine(""</br>"")")
        txtstream.WriteLine("    txtstream.WriteLine(""<h1 nowrap='nowrap'
STYLE=""""""background-color:white;FONT-WEIGHT:normal; FONT-SIZE: 48px;
COLOR: navy; FONT-STYLE: normal; FONT-FAMILY: Edwardian Script
ITC"""""">PlanetMPs  </H1>"")")
        txtstream.WriteLine("    txtstream.WriteLine(""</br>"")")


    Select Case TableType

        Case "Reports"

            txtstream.WriteLine("    txtstream.WriteLine(""<table border=0
cellspacing=3 cellpadding=3>"")")

        Case "Tables"
```

```vb
        txtstream.WriteLine("    txtstream.WriteLine(""""<table
style='border:Double;border-width:1px;border-color:navy;' rules=all frames=both
cellpadding=2 cellspacing=2 Width=0>""")")

    End Select

  End Sub


  Private Sub Write_The_HTML_Code()


        txtstream.WriteLine("    Set ws = CreateObject("""WScript.Shell""")")
        txtstream.WriteLine("    Set fso =
CreateObject("""Scripting.FileSystemObject""")")
        txtstream.WriteLine("    Set txtstream = fso.OpenTextFile(ws.CurrentDirectory +
"""\" & Tablename & ".html""", 2, True, -2)")
        txtstream.WriteLine("    txtstream.WriteLine(""""<hmtl>""")")
        txtstream.WriteLine("    txtstream.WriteLine(""""<head>""")")
        txtstream.WriteLine("    txtstream.WriteLine(""""<title>""" & Tablename &
"""</title>""")")
        Add_StyleSheet()
        txtstream.WriteLine("    txtstream.WriteLine(""""<body>""")")
        txtstream.WriteLine("    txtstream.WriteLine(""""<center>""")")
        txtstream.WriteLine("    txtstream.WriteLine(""""</br>""")")
        txtstream.WriteLine("    txtstream.WriteLine(""""<h1 nowrap='nowrap'
STYLE="""""""background-color:white;FONT-WEIGHT:normal; FONT-SIZE: 48px;
COLOR: navy; FONT-STYLE: normal; FONT-FAMILY: Edwardian Script
ITC"""""">PlanetMPs  </H1>""")")
        txtstream.WriteLine("    txtstream.WriteLine(""""</br>""")")


    Select Case TableType

        Case "Reports"

            txtstream.WriteLine("    txtstream.WriteLine(""""<table border=0
cellspacing=3 cellpadding=3>""")")

        Case "Tables"

            txtstream.WriteLine("    txtstream.WriteLine(""""<table
style='border:Double;border-width:1px;border-color:navy;' rules=all frames=both
cellpadding=2 cellspacing=2 Width=0>""")")

    End Select

  End Sub
```

The ASP, ASPX enumeration code

This routine is providing you both horizontal and vertical orientation and additional rendering controls:

```
Private Sub Write_The_ASP_Enumerator_Code()

    Select Case Orientation

        Case "Horizontal"

            If StyleSheet = "In Line" Then

                txtstream.WriteLine("
txtstream.WriteLine(""""Response.Write(""""""""<tr>"""""""" & vbcrlf)"")")
                txtstream.WriteLine("    For x = 0 To rs.Fields.Count - 1")
                txtstream.WriteLine("
txtstream.WriteLine(""""Response.Write(""""""""<th style="""""""" font-family:Calibri,
Sans-Serif;font-size: 12px;color:darkred;"""""""" align='left' nowrap='nowrap'>"""" &
rs.Fields(x).Name & """"</th>"""""""" & vbcrlf)"""")")
                txtstream.WriteLine("    Next")
                txtstream.WriteLine("
txtstream.WriteLine(""""Response.Write(""""""""</tr>"""""""" & vbcrlf)"")")
                txtstream.WriteLine("""")
                txtstream.WriteLine("    Do While (rs.Eof = False)")
```

```vbnet
            txtstream.WriteLine("
txtstream.WriteLine(""Response.Write("""""<tr>"""" & vbcrlf)"")")
            txtstream.WriteLine("      For x = 0 To rs.Fields.Count - 1")


       Select Case ControlType

          Case "None"

              txtstream.WriteLine("
txtstream.WriteLine(""Response.Write(""""""<td style="""""""font-family:Calibri,
Sans-Serif;font-size: 12px;color:navy;"""""" align='left' nowrap='nowrap'>"" &
rs.Fields(x).Value & ""</td>"""""" & vbcrlf)"")")

          Case "Button"

              txtstream.WriteLine("
txtstream.WriteLine(""Response.Write(""""""<td style="""""""font-family:Calibri,
Sans-Serif;font-size: 12px;color:navy;"""""" align='left' nowrap='true'><button
style='width:100%;' value ="""" & rs.Fields(x).Value & """>"" & rs.Fields(x).Value &
""</button></td>"""""" & vbcrlf)"")")

          Case "Checkbox"

              txtstream.WriteLine("
txtstream.WriteLine(""Response.Write(""""""<td style="""""""font-family:Calibri,
Sans-Serif;font-size: 12px;color:navy;"""""" align='left' nowrap='true'><input
type=Checkbox value="""""""""" & rs.Fields(x).Value & """""""""""></input></td>"""""" &
vbcrlf)"")")

          Case "Combobox"

              txtstream.WriteLine("
txtstream.WriteLine(""Response.Write(""""""<td style="""""""font-family:Calibri,
Sans-Serif;font-size: 12px;color:navy;"""""" align='left'
nowrap='true'><select><option value = """""""""" & rs.Fields(x).Value & """""""""">"" &
rs.Fields(x).Value & ""</option></select></td>"""""" & vbcrlf)"")")

          Case "Div"

              txtstream.WriteLine("
txtstream.WriteLine(""Response.Write(""""""<td style="""""""font-family:Calibri,
Sans-Serif;font-size: 12px;color:navy;"""""" align='left' nowrap='true'><div>"" &
rs.Fields(x).Value & ""</div></td>"""""" & vbcrlf)"")")

          Case "Link"

              txtstream.WriteLine("
txtstream.WriteLine(""Response.Write(""""""<td style="""""""font-family:Calibri,
```

```
Sans-Serif;font-size: 12px;color:navy;""""" align='left' nowrap='true'><a href='""" &
rs.Fields(x).Value & ""'>"" & rs.Fields(x).Value & ""</a></td>"""""" & vbcrlf)""")")

            Case "Listbox"

                txtstream.WriteLine("
txtstream.WriteLine(""Response.Write(""""""<td style="""""font-family:Calibri,
Sans-Serif;font-size: 12px;color:navy;""""" align='left' nowrap='true'><select
multiple><option value = """""""" & rs.Fields(x).Value & """""""">"" &
rs.Fields(x).Value & ""</option></select></td>"""""" & vbcrlf)""")")

            Case "Span"

                txtstream.WriteLine("
txtstream.WriteLine(""Response.Write(""""""<td style="""""font-family:Calibri,
Sans-Serif;font-size: 12px;color:navy;""""" align='left' nowrap='true'><span>"" &
rs.Fields(x).Value & ""</span></td>"""""" & vbcrlf)""")")

            Case "Textarea"

                txtstream.WriteLine("
txtstream.WriteLine(""Response.Write(""""""<td style="""""font-family:Calibri,
Sans-Serif;font-size: 12px;color:navy;""""" align='left' nowrap='true'><textarea>""
& rs.Fields(x).Value & ""</textarea></td>"""""" & vbcrlf)""")")

            Case "Textbox"

                txtstream.WriteLine("
txtstream.WriteLine(""Response.Write(""""""<td style="""""font-family:Calibri,
Sans-Serif;font-size: 12px;color:navy;""""" align='left' nowrap='true'><input
type=text value="""""""" & rs.Fields(x).Value & """""""""></input></td>"""""" &
vbcrlf)""")")

        End Select


            txtstream.WriteLine("        Next")
            txtstream.WriteLine("
txtstream.WriteLine(""Response.Write(""""""</tr>"""""" & vbcrlf)""")")
            txtstream.WriteLine("        rs.MoveNext")
            txtstream.WriteLine("    Loop")

        Else


            txtstream.WriteLine("
txtstream.WriteLine(""Response.Write(""""""<tr>"""""" & vbcrlf)""")")
            txtstream.WriteLine("    For x = 0 To rs.Fields.Count - 1")
```

```vb
        txtstream.WriteLine("
txtstream.WriteLine(""""Response.Write("""""""<th align='left' nowrap='nowrap'>"" &
rs.Fields(x).Name & ""</th>"""""" & vbcrlf)"""")")
        txtstream.WriteLine("    Next")
        txtstream.WriteLine("
txtstream.WriteLine(""""Response.Write("""""""</tr>"""""" & vbcrlf)"""")")
        txtstream.WriteLine("")
        txtstream.WriteLine("    Do While (rs.Eof = False)")
        txtstream.WriteLine("
txtstream.WriteLine(""""Response.Write("""""""<tr>"""""" & vbcrlf)"""")")
        txtstream.WriteLine("        For x = 0 To rs.Fields.Count - 1")

    Select Case ControlType

        Case "None"

            txtstream.WriteLine("
txtstream.WriteLine(""""Response.Write("""""""<td align='left' nowrap='nowrap'>"" &
rs.Fields(x).Value & ""</td>"""""" & vbcrlf)"""")")

        Case "Button"

            txtstream.WriteLine("
txtstream.WriteLine(""""Response.Write("""""""<td align='left' nowrap='true'><button
style='width:100%;' value ="""" & rs.Fields(x).Value & """">"" & rs.Fields(x).Value &
""</button></td>"""""" & vbcrlf)"""")")

        Case "Checkbox"

            txtstream.WriteLine("
txtstream.WriteLine(""""Response.Write("""""""<td align='left' nowrap='true'><input
type=Checkbox value="""""""""" & rs.Fields(x).Value & """"""""""></input></td>"""""" &
vbcrlf)"""")")

        Case "Combobox"

            txtstream.WriteLine("
txtstream.WriteLine(""""Response.Write("""""""<td align='left'
nowrap='true'><select><option value = """"""""""" & rs.Fields(x).Value & """"""""""">"" &
rs.Fields(x).Value & ""</option></select></td>"""""" & vbcrlf)"""")")

        Case "Div"

            txtstream.WriteLine("
txtstream.WriteLine(""""Response.Write("""""""<td align='left' nowrap='true'><div>""""
& rs.Fields(x).Value & ""</div></td>"""""" & vbcrlf)"""")")

        Case "Link"
```

```
            txtstream.WriteLine("
txtstream.WriteLine(""Response.Write(""""""<td  align='left' nowrap='true'><a
href=''" & rs.Fields(x).Value & """'>"" & rs.Fields(x).Value & ""</a></td>"""""" &
vbcrlf)"")")

                Case "Listbox"

            txtstream.WriteLine("
txtstream.WriteLine(""Response.Write(""""""<td  align='left' nowrap='true'><select
multiple><option value = """""""" & rs.Fields(x).Value & """"""""">"" &
rs.Fields(x).Value & ""</option></select></td>"""""" & vbcrlf)"")")

                Case "Span"

            txtstream.WriteLine("
txtstream.WriteLine(""Response.Write(""""""<td  align='left'
nowrap='true'><span>"" & rs.Fields(x).Value & ""</span></td>"""""" & vbcrlf)"")")

                Case "Textarea"

            txtstream.WriteLine("
txtstream.WriteLine(""Response.Write(""""""<td  align='left'
nowrap='true'><textarea>"" & rs.Fields(x).Value & ""</textarea></td>"""""" &
vbcrlf)"")")

                Case "Textbox"

            txtstream.WriteLine("
txtstream.WriteLine(""Response.Write(""""""<td  align='left' nowrap='true'><input
type=text value="""""""""" & rs.Fields(x).Value & """""""""></input></td>"""""" &
vbcrlf)"")")

                End Select


            txtstream.WriteLine("          Next")
            txtstream.WriteLine("
txtstream.WriteLine(""Response.Write(""""""</tr>"""""" & vbcrlf)"")")
            txtstream.WriteLine("          rs.MoveNext")
            txtstream.WriteLine("     Loop")


            End If


        Case "Vertical"


            If StyleSheet = "In Line" Then
```

```vb
        txtstream.WriteLine("    For x = 0 To rs.Fields.Count - 1")

        txtstream.WriteLine("
txtstream.WriteLine(""""Response.Write("""""""<tr><th style="""""" font-family:Calibri,
Sans-Serif;font-size: 12px;color:darkred;"""""" align='left' nowrap='nowrap'>"" &
rs.Fields(x).Name & ""</th>"""""" & vbcrlf)"")")

        txtstream.WriteLine("    rs.MoveFirst()")

        txtstream.WriteLine("    Do While (rs.Eof = False)")

        txtstream.WriteLine("
txtstream.WriteLine(""""Response.Write("""""""<td style=""""""font-family:Calibri,
Sans-Serif;font-size: 12px;color:navy;"""""">"" & rs.Fields(x).Value & ""</td>"""""" &
vbcrlf)"")")

            Select Case ControlType

                Case "None"

        txtstream.WriteLine("
txtstream.WriteLine(""""Response.Write("""""""<td style=""""""font-family:Calibri,
Sans-Serif;font-size: 12px;color:navy;"""""" align='left' nowrap='nowrap'>"" &
rs.Fields(x).Value & ""</td>"""""" & vbcrlf)"")")

                Case "Button"

        txtstream.WriteLine("
txtstream.WriteLine(""""Response.Write("""""""<td style=""""""font-family:Calibri,
Sans-Serif;font-size: 12px;color:navy;"""""" align='left' nowrap='true'><button
style='width:100%;' value ='"" & rs.Fields(x).Value & "">"" & rs.Fields(x).Value &
""</button></td>"""""" & vbcrlf)"")")

                Case "Checkbox"

        txtstream.WriteLine("
txtstream.WriteLine(""""Response.Write("""""""<td style=""""""font-family:Calibri,
Sans-Serif;font-size: 12px;color:navy;"""""" align='left' nowrap='true'><input
type=Checkbox value="""""""""" & rs.Fields(x).Value & """"""""></input></td>"""""" &
vbcrlf)"")")

                Case "Combobox"

        txtstream.WriteLine("
txtstream.WriteLine(""""Response.Write("""""""<td style=""""""font-family:Calibri,
Sans-Serif;font-size: 12px;color:navy;"""""" align='left'
nowrap='true'><select><option value = """""""""" & rs.Fields(x).Value & """"""""">"" &
rs.Fields(x).Value & ""</option></select></td>"""""" & vbcrlf)"")")
```

```
        Case "Div"

            txtstream.WriteLine("
txtstream.WriteLine(""""Response.Write(""""""<td style=""""""font-family:Calibri,
Sans-Serif;font-size: 12px;color:navy;"""""" align='left' nowrap='true'><div>"" &
rs.Fields(x).Value & ""</div></td>"""""" & vbcrlf)"")")

        Case "Link"

            txtstream.WriteLine("
txtstream.WriteLine(""""Response.Write(""""""<td style=""""""font-family:Calibri,
Sans-Serif;font-size: 12px;color:navy;"""""" align='left' nowrap='true'><a href='"" &
rs.Fields(x).Value & "">"" & rs.Fields(x).Value & ""</a></td>"""""" & vbcrlf)"")")

        Case "Listbox"

            txtstream.WriteLine("
txtstream.WriteLine(""""Response.Write(""""""<td style=""""""font-family:Calibri,
Sans-Serif;font-size: 12px;color:navy;"""""" align='left' nowrap='true'><select
multiple><option value = """""""" & rs.Fields(x).Value & """""""">"" &
rs.Fields(x).Value & ""</option></select></td>"""""" & vbcrlf)"")")

        Case "Span"

            txtstream.WriteLine("
txtstream.WriteLine(""""Response.Write(""""""<td style=""""""font-family:Calibri,
Sans-Serif;font-size: 12px;color:navy;"""""" align='left' nowrap='true'><span>"" &
rs.Fields(x).Value & ""</span></td>"""""" & vbcrlf)"")")

        Case "Textarea"

            txtstream.WriteLine("
txtstream.WriteLine(""""Response.Write(""""""<td style=""""""font-family:Calibri,
Sans-Serif;font-size: 12px;color:navy;"""""" align='left' nowrap='true'><textarea>""
& rs.Fields(x).Value & ""</textarea></td>"""""" & vbcrlf)"")")

        Case "Textbox"

            txtstream.WriteLine("
txtstream.WriteLine(""""Response.Write(""""""<td style=""""""font-family:Calibri,
Sans-Serif;font-size: 12px;color:navy;"""""" align='left' nowrap='true'><input
type=text value="""""""" & rs.Fields(x).Value & """""""""></input></td>"""""" &
vbcrlf)"")")

    End Select

        txtstream.WriteLine("        rs.MoveNext")
        txtstream.WriteLine("    Loop")
        txtstream.WriteLine("
txtstream.WriteLine(""""Response.Write(""""""</tr>"""""" & vbcrlf)"")")
```

```vb
        txtstream.WriteLine("      Next")

    Else

        txtstream.WriteLine("      For x = 0 To rs.Fields.Count - 1")

        txtstream.WriteLine("
txtstream.WriteLine(""""Response.Write(""""""""<tr><th align='left'
nowrap='nowrap'>"" & rs.Fields(x).Name & ""</th>"""""""" & vbcrlf)"""")")

        txtstream.WriteLine("       rs.MoveFirst()")

        txtstream.WriteLine("       Do While (rs.Eof = False)")


    Select Case ControlType

        Case "None"

            txtstream.WriteLine("
txtstream.WriteLine(""""Response.Write(""""""""<td  align='left' nowrap='nowrap'>"" &
rs.Fields(x).Value & ""</td>"""""""" & vbcrlf)"""")")

        Case "Button"

            txtstream.WriteLine("
txtstream.WriteLine(""""Response.Write(""""""""<td  align='left' nowrap='true'><button
style='width:100%;' value ='"" & rs.Fields(x).Value & "">"" & rs.Fields(x).Value &
""</button></td>"""""""" & vbcrlf)"""")")

        Case "Checkbox"

            txtstream.WriteLine("
txtstream.WriteLine(""""Response.Write(""""""""<td  align='left' nowrap='true'><input
type=Checkbox value=""""""""""" & rs.Fields(x).Value & """""""""""></input></td>"""""""" &
vbcrlf)"""")")

        Case "Combobox"

            txtstream.WriteLine("
txtstream.WriteLine(""""Response.Write(""""""""<td  align='left'
nowrap='true'><select><option value = """""""""" & rs.Fields(x).Value & """"""""""">"" &
rs.Fields(x).Value & ""</option></select></td>"""""""" & vbcrlf)"""")")

        Case "Div"

            txtstream.WriteLine("
txtstream.WriteLine(""""Response.Write(""""""""<td  align='left' nowrap='true'><div>""
& rs.Fields(x).Value & ""</div></td>"""""""" & vbcrlf)"""")")
```

```vb
            Case "Link"

                txtstream.WriteLine("
txtstream.WriteLine("""Response.Write(""""""<td  align='left' nowrap='true'><a
href='""" & rs.Fields(x).Value & """'>""" & rs.Fields(x).Value & """</a></td>"""""" &
vbcrlf)""")")

            Case "Listbox"

                txtstream.WriteLine("
txtstream.WriteLine("""Response.Write(""""""<td  align='left' nowrap='true'><select
multiple><option value = """""""" & rs.Fields(x).Value & """"""""">""" &
rs.Fields(x).Value & """</option></select></td>"""""" & vbcrlf)""")")

            Case "Span"

                txtstream.WriteLine("
txtstream.WriteLine("""Response.Write(""""""<td  align='left'
nowrap='true'><span>""" & rs.Fields(x).Value & """</span></td>"""""" & vbcrlf)""")")

            Case "Textarea"

                txtstream.WriteLine("
txtstream.WriteLine("""Response.Write(""""""<td  align='left'
nowrap='true'><textarea>""" & rs.Fields(x).Value & """</textarea></td>"""""" &
vbcrlf)""")")

            Case "Textbox"

                txtstream.WriteLine("
txtstream.WriteLine("""Response.Write(""""""<td  align='left' nowrap='true'><input
type=text value="""""""" & rs.Fields(x).Value & """""""""></input></td>"""""" &
vbcrlf)""")")

        End Select

            txtstream.WriteLine("        rs.MoveNext")
            txtstream.WriteLine("      Loop")
            txtstream.WriteLine("
txtstream.WriteLine("""Response.Write(""""""</tr>"""""" & vbcrlf)""")")
            txtstream.WriteLine("  Next")


        End If


    End Select
```

End Sub

The HTA and HTML enumeration code

This routine is providing you both horizontal and vertical orientation and additional rendering controls:

```
Private Sub Write_The_HTML_Enumerator_Code()

    Select Case Orientation

        Case "Horizontal"

            If StyleSheet = "In Line" Then

                txtstream.WriteLine("    txtstream.WriteLine(""<tr>"")")
                txtstream.WriteLine("    For x = 0 To rs.Fields.Count - 1")
                txtstream.WriteLine("        txtstream.WriteLine(""<th style=""""" font-family:Calibri, Sans-Serif;font-size: 12px;color:darkred;""""" align='left' nowrap='nowrap'>"" & rs.Fields(x).Name & ""</th>"")")
                txtstream.WriteLine("    Next")
```

```
txtstream.WriteLine("    txtstream.WriteLine(""</tr>"")")
txtstream.WriteLine("")
txtstream.WriteLine("    Do While (rs.Eof = False)")
txtstream.WriteLine("        txtstream.WriteLine(""<tr>"")")
txtstream.WriteLine("        For x = 0 To rs.Fields.Count - 1")


        Select Case ControlType

            Case "None"

                txtstream.WriteLine("          txtstream.WriteLine(""<td
style="""""font-family:Calibri, Sans-Serif;font-size: 12px;color:navy;""""""
align='left' nowrap='nowrap'>"" & rs.Fields(x).Value & ""</td>"")")

            Case "Button"

                txtstream.WriteLine("          txtstream.WriteLine(""<td
style="""""font-family:Calibri, Sans-Serif;font-size: 12px;color:navy;""""""
align='left' nowrap='true'><button style='width:100%;' value ='"" &
rs.Fields(x).Value & "">"" & rs.Fields(x).Value & ""</button></td>"")")

            Case "Checkbox"

                txtstream.WriteLine("          txtstream.WriteLine(""<td
style="""""font-family:Calibri, Sans-Serif;font-size: 12px;color:navy;""""""
align='left' nowrap='true'><input type=Checkbox value="""""""" & rs.Fields(x).Value
& """"""""></input></td>"")")

            Case "Combobox"

                txtstream.WriteLine("          txtstream.WriteLine(""<td
style="""""font-family:Calibri, Sans-Serif;font-size: 12px;color:navy;""""""
align='left' nowrap='true'><select><option value = """""""" & rs.Fields(x).Value &
""""""">"" & rs.Fields(x).Value & ""</option></select></td>"")")

            Case "Div"

                txtstream.WriteLine("          txtstream.WriteLine(""<td
style="""""font-family:Calibri, Sans-Serif;font-size: 12px;color:navy;""""""
align='left' nowrap='true'><div>"" & rs.Fields(x).Value & ""</div></td>"")")

            Case "Link"

                txtstream.WriteLine("          txtstream.WriteLine(""<td
style="""""font-family:Calibri, Sans-Serif;font-size: 12px;color:navy;""""""
align='left' nowrap='true'><a href='"" & rs.Fields(x).Value & "">"" &
rs.Fields(x).Value & ""</a></td>"")")

            Case "Listbox"
```

```
                txtstream.WriteLine("           txtstream.WriteLine(""<td
style="""""font-family:Calibri, Sans-Serif;font-size: 12px;color:navy;"""""
align='left' nowrap='true'><select multiple><option value = """"""" &
rs.Fields(x).Value & """"""">"" & rs.Fields(x).Value &
""</option></select></td>"")")

            Case "Span"

                txtstream.WriteLine("           txtstream.WriteLine(""<td
style="""""font-family:Calibri, Sans-Serif;font-size: 12px;color:navy;"""""
align='left' nowrap='true'><span>"" & rs.Fields(x).Value & ""</span></td>"")")

            Case "Textarea"

                txtstream.WriteLine("           txtstream.WriteLine(""<td
style="""""font-family:Calibri, Sans-Serif;font-size: 12px;color:navy;"""""
align='left' nowrap='true'><textarea>"" & rs.Fields(x).Value &
""</textarea></td>"")")

            Case "Textbox"

                txtstream.WriteLine("           txtstream.WriteLine(""<td
style="""""font-family:Calibri, Sans-Serif;font-size: 12px;color:navy;"""""
align='left' nowrap='true'><input type=text value="""""""" & rs.Fields(x).Value &
""""""""></input></td>"")")

        End Select


        txtstream.WriteLine("       Next")
        txtstream.WriteLine("       txtstream.WriteLine(""</tr>"")")
        txtstream.WriteLine("       rs.MoveNext")
        txtstream.WriteLine("   Loop")

    Else


        txtstream.WriteLine("     txtstream.WriteLine(""<tr>"")")
        txtstream.WriteLine("     For x = 0 To rs.Fields.Count - 1")
        txtstream.WriteLine("         txtstream.WriteLine(""<th align='left'
nowrap-'nowrap'>"" & rs.Fields(x).Name & ""</th>"")")
        txtstream.WriteLine("     Next")
        txtstream.WriteLine("     txtstream.WriteLine(""</tr>"")")
        txtstream.WriteLine("")
        txtstream.WriteLine("   Do While (rs.Eof = False)")
        txtstream.WriteLine("       txtstream.WriteLine(""<tr>"")")
        txtstream.WriteLine("       For x = 0 To rs.Fields.Count - 1")
```

```vb
Select Case ControlType

    Case "None"

        txtstream.WriteLine("        txtstream.WriteLine(""""<td
align='left' nowrap='nowrap'>""" & rs.Fields(x).Value & """</td>"""")")

    Case "Button"

        txtstream.WriteLine("        txtstream.WriteLine(""""<td
align='left' nowrap='true'><button style='width:100%;' value =""""" &
rs.Fields(x).Value & """"">""" & rs.Fields(x).Value & """</button></td>"""")")

    Case "Checkbox"

        txtstream.WriteLine("        txtstream.WriteLine(""""<td
align='left' nowrap='true'><input type=Checkbox value="""""""" & rs.Fields(x).Value
& """"""""></input></td>"""")")

    Case "Combobox"

        txtstream.WriteLine("        txtstream.WriteLine(""""<td
align='left' nowrap='true'><select><option value = """""""" & rs.Fields(x).Value &
""""""""">""" & rs.Fields(x).Value & """</option></select></td>"""")")

    Case "Div"

        txtstream.WriteLine("        txtstream.WriteLine(""""<td
align='left' nowrap='true'><div>""" & rs.Fields(x).Value & """</div></td>"""")")

    Case "Link"

        txtstream.WriteLine("        txtstream.WriteLine(""""<td
align='left' nowrap='true'><a href=""""" & rs.Fields(x).Value & """"">""" &
rs.Fields(x).Value & """</a></td>"""")")

    Case "Listbox"

        txtstream.WriteLine("        txtstream.WriteLine(""""<td
align='left' nowrap='true'><select multiple><option value = """""""" &
rs.Fields(x).Value & """"""""">""" & rs.Fields(x).Value &
"""</option></select></td>"""")")

    Case "Span"

        txtstream.WriteLine("        txtstream.WriteLine(""""<td
align='left' nowrap='true'><span>""" & rs.Fields(x).Value & """</span></td>"""")")

    Case "Textarea"
```

```
                    txtstream.WriteLine("          txtstream.WriteLine(""""<td
align='left' nowrap='true'><textarea>"""" & rs.Fields(x).Value &
""""</textarea></td>"""")")

              Case "Textbox"

                    txtstream.WriteLine("          txtstream.WriteLine(""""<td
align='left' nowrap='true'><input type=text value=""""""""""" & rs.Fields(x).Value &
"""""""""""></input></td>"""")")

              End Select


                    txtstream.WriteLine("      Next")
                    txtstream.WriteLine("          txtstream.WriteLine(""""</tr>"""")")
                    txtstream.WriteLine("          rs.MoveNext")
                    txtstream.WriteLine("    Loop")


       End If


   Case "Vertical"


       If StyleSheet = "In Line" Then

          txtstream.WriteLine("    For x = 0 To rs.Fields.Count - 1")

              txtstream.WriteLine("          txtstream.WriteLine(""""<tr><th style="""""""""
font-family:Calibri, Sans-Serif;font-size: 12px;color:darkred;""""""""" align='left'
nowrap='nowrap'>"""" & rs.Fields(x).Name & """"</th>"""")")

              txtstream.WriteLine("          rs.MoveFirst()")

              txtstream.WriteLine("          Do While (rs.Eof = False)")

              txtstream.WriteLine("          txtstream.WriteLine(""""<td style="""""""""font-
family:Calibri, Sans-Serif;font-size: 12px;color:navy;""""""""">"""" & rs.Fields(x).Value &
""""</td>"""")")

                Select Case ControlType

                Case "None"

                    txtstream.WriteLine("          txtstream.WriteLine(""""<td
style="""""""""font-family:Calibri, Sans-Serif;font-size: 12px;color:navy;"""""""""
align='left' nowrap='nowrap'>"""" & rs.Fields(x).Value & """"</td>"""")")
```

```vb
            Case "Button"

                txtstream.WriteLine("          txtstream.WriteLine(""""<td
style="""""""font-family:Calibri, Sans-Serif;font-size: 12px;color:navy;"""""""
align='left' nowrap='true'><button style='width:100%;' value ='""" &
rs.Fields(x).Value & """">""" & rs.Fields(x).Value & ""</button></td>""")")

            Case "Checkbox"

                txtstream.WriteLine("          txtstream.WriteLine(""""<td
style="""""""font-family:Calibri, Sans-Serif;font-size: 12px;color:navy;"""""""
align='left' nowrap='true'><input type=Checkbox value="""""""" & rs.Fields(x).Value
& """"""""></input></td>""")")

            Case "Combobox"

                txtstream.WriteLine("          txtstream.WriteLine(""""<td
style="""""""font-family:Calibri, Sans-Serif;font-size: 12px;color:navy;"""""""
align='left' nowrap='true'><select><option value = """""""" & rs.Fields(x).Value &
""""""""">""" & rs.Fields(x).Value & ""</option></select></td>""")")

            Case "Div"

                txtstream.WriteLine("          txtstream.WriteLine(""""<td
style="""""""font-family:Calibri, Sans-Serif;font-size: 12px;color:navy;"""""""
align='left' nowrap='true'><div>""" & rs.Fields(x).Value & ""</div></td>""")")

            Case "Link"

                txtstream.WriteLine("          txtstream.WriteLine(""""<td
style="""""""font-family:Calibri, Sans-Serif;font-size: 12px;color:navy;"""""""
align='left' nowrap='true'><a href='""" & rs.Fields(x).Value & """">""" &
rs.Fields(x).Value & ""</a></td>""")")

            Case "Listbox"

                txtstream.WriteLine("          txtstream.WriteLine(""""<td
style="""""""font-family:Calibri, Sans-Serif;font-size: 12px;color:navy;"""""""
align='left' nowrap='true'><select multiple><option value = """""""" &
rs.Fields(x).Value & """"""""">""" & rs.Fields(x).Value &
""</option></select></td>""")")

            Case "Span"

                txtstream.WriteLine("          txtstream.WriteLine(""""<td
style="""""""font-family:Calibri, Sans-Serif;font-size: 12px;color:navy;"""""""
align='left' nowrap='true'><span>""" & rs.Fields(x).Value & ""</span></td>""")")

            Case "Textarea"
```

```
                    txtstream.WriteLine("        txtstream.WriteLine(""""<td
style="""""font-family:Calibri, Sans-Serif;font-size: 12px;color:navy;"""""
align='left' nowrap='true'><textarea>"""" & rs.Fields(x).Value &
""""</textarea></td>"""")")

            Case "Textbox"

                    txtstream.WriteLine("        txtstream.WriteLine(""""<td
style="""""font-family:Calibri, Sans-Serif;font-size: 12px;color:navy;"""""
align='left' nowrap='true'><input type=text value="""""""" & rs.Fields(x).Value &
""""""""></input></td>"""")")

            End Select

            txtstream.WriteLine("        rs.MoveNext")
            txtstream.WriteLine("    Loop")
            txtstream.WriteLine("        txtstream.WriteLine(""""</tr>"""")")
            txtstream.WriteLine("    Next")


        Else

            txtstream.WriteLine("    For x = 0 To rs.Fields.Count - 1")

            txtstream.WriteLine("        txtstream.WriteLine(""""<tr><th align='left'
nowrap='nowrap'>"""" & rs.Fields(x).Name & """"</th>"""")")

            txtstream.WriteLine("    rs.MoveFirst()")

            txtstream.WriteLine("    Do While (rs.Eof = False)")


        Select Case ControlType

            Case "None"

                    txtstream.WriteLine("        txtstream.WriteLine(""""<td
align='left' nowrap='nowrap'>"""" & rs.Fields(x).Value & """"</td>"""")")

            Case "Button"

                    txtstream.WriteLine("        txtstream.WriteLine(""""<td
align='left' nowrap='true'><button style='width:100%;' value ='"""" &
rs.Fields(x).Value & """">"""" & rs.Fields(x).Value & """"</button></td>"""")")

            Case "Checkbox"

                    txtstream.WriteLine("        txtstream.WriteLine(""""<td
align='left' nowrap='true'><input type=Checkbox value="""""""" & rs.Fields(x).Value
& """"""""></input></td>"""")")
```

```vbscript
                Case "Combobox"

                    txtstream.WriteLine("        txtstream.WriteLine(""""<td
align='left' nowrap='true'><select><option value = """""""""" & rs.Fields(x).Value &
"""""""""">"""" & rs.Fields(x).Value & """"</option></select></td>"""")")

                Case "Div"

                    txtstream.WriteLine("        txtstream.WriteLine(""""<td
align='left' nowrap='true'><div>"""" & rs.Fields(x).Value & """"</div></td>"""")")

                Case "Link"

                    txtstream.WriteLine("        txtstream.WriteLine(""""<td
align='left' nowrap='true'><a href='""""" & rs.Fields(x).Value & """"'>"""" &
rs.Fields(x).Value & """"</a></td>"""")")

                Case "Listbox"

                    txtstream.WriteLine("        txtstream.WriteLine(""""<td
align='left' nowrap='true'><select multiple><option value = """""""""" &
rs.Fields(x).Value & """"""""""">"""" & rs.Fields(x).Value &
""""</option></select></td>"""")")

                Case "Span"

                    txtstream.WriteLine("        txtstream.WriteLine(""""<td
align='left' nowrap='true'><span>"""" & rs.Fields(x).Value & """"</span></td>"""")")

                Case "Textarea"

                    txtstream.WriteLine("        txtstream.WriteLine(""""<td
align='left' nowrap='true'><textarea>"""" & rs.Fields(x).Value &
""""</textarea></td>"""")")

                Case "Textbox"

                    txtstream.WriteLine("        txtstream.WriteLine(""""<td
align='left' nowrap='true'><input type=text value=""""""""" & rs.Fields(x).Value &
"""""""""></input></td>"""")")

            End Select

            txtstream.WriteLine("        rs.MoveNext")
            txtstream.WriteLine("    Loop")
            txtstream.WriteLine("    txtstream.WriteLine(""""</tr>"""")")
            txtstream.WriteLine("  Next")
```

```
        End If

    End Select

End Sub
```

The various text file delimited files

This routine is providing you both horizontal and vertical orientation:

Private Sub Do_Colon_Delimited_Code()

```
    txtstream.WriteLine("    Set ws = CreateObject(""WScript.Shell"")")
    txtstream.WriteLine("    Set fso =
CreateObject(""Scripting.FileSystemObject"")")
    txtstream.WriteLine("    Set txtstream = fso.OpenTextFile(ws.CurrentDirectory +
""\" & Tablename & ".txt""", 2, True, -2)")

    txtstream.WriteLine("    Dim tstr")
    txtstream.WriteLine("    tstr= """""" ")

Select Case Orientation

    Case "Horizontal"

        txtstream.WriteLine("    For x = 0 To rs.Fields.Count - 1")
        txtstream.WriteLine("     If (tstr <> """""") Then")
        txtstream.WriteLine("      tstr = tstr + "".""" ")
        txtstream.WriteLine("     End If")
        txtstream.WriteLine("     tstr = tstr + rs.Fields(x).Name")
        txtstream.WriteLine("    Next")
        txtstream.WriteLine("    txtstream.Writeline(tstr)")
```

```
            txtstream.WriteLine("    tstr = """"" ")
            txtstream.WriteLine("    rs.MoveFirst()")
            txtstream.WriteLine("    Do While (rs.EOF = False)")
            txtstream.WriteLine("      For x = 0 To rs.Fields.Count - 1")
            txtstream.WriteLine("        If (tstr <> """"") Then")
            txtstream.WriteLine("          tstr = tstr + "":"" ")
            txtstream.WriteLine("        End If")
            txtstream.WriteLine("        tstr = tstr & chr(34) & rs.Fields(x).Value &
chr(34)")
            txtstream.WriteLine("      Next")
            txtstream.WriteLine("      txtstream.Writeline(tstr)")
            txtstream.WriteLine("      tstr = """"" ")
            txtstream.WriteLine("      rs.MoveNext")
            txtstream.WriteLine("    Loop")


        Case "Vertical"


            txtstream.WriteLine("    For x = 0 To rs.Fields.Count - 1")
            txtstream.WriteLine("      tstr = rs.Fields(x).Name")
            txtstream.WriteLine("      rs.MoveFirst()")
            txtstream.WriteLine("      Do While (rs.EOF = False)")
            txtstream.WriteLine("        If (tstr <> """"") Then")
            txtstream.WriteLine("          tstr = tstr + "":"" ")
            txtstream.WriteLine("        End If")
            txtstream.WriteLine("        tstr = tstr & chr(34) & rs.Fields(x).Value &
chr(34)")
            txtstream.WriteLine("        rs.MoveNext")
            txtstream.WriteLine("      Loop")
            txtstream.WriteLine("      txtstream.Writeline(tstr)")
            txtstream.WriteLine("      tstr = """"" ")
            txtstream.WriteLine("    Next")



    End Select

    txtstream.WriteLine("")
    txtstream.WriteLine("        txtstream.Close")
    txtstream.WriteLine("")


End Sub
```

```vb
Private Sub Do_CSV_Code()

    txtstream.WriteLine("    Set ws = CreateObject(""WScript.Shell"")")
    txtstream.WriteLine("    Set fso =
CreateObject(""Scripting.FileSystemObject"")")
    txtstream.WriteLine("    Set txtstream = fso.OpenTextFile(ws.CurrentDirectory +
""\" & Tablename & ".csv""", 2, True, -2)")

    txtstream.WriteLine("    Dim tstr")
    txtstream.WriteLine("    tstr= """""" ")

    Select Case Orientation

        Case "Horizontal"

            txtstream.WriteLine("    For x = 0 To rs.Fields.Count - 1")
            txtstream.WriteLine("        If (tstr <> """""") Then")
            txtstream.WriteLine("            tstr = tstr + "","""" ")
            txtstream.WriteLine("        End If")
            txtstream.WriteLine("        tstr = tstr + rs.Fields(x).Name")
            txtstream.WriteLine("    Next")
            txtstream.WriteLine("    txtstream.Writeline(tstr)")
            txtstream.WriteLine("    tstr = """""" ")
            txtstream.WriteLine("    rs.MoveFirst()")
            txtstream.WriteLine("    Do While (rs.EOF = False)")
            txtstream.WriteLine("        For x = 0 To rs.Fields.Count - 1")
            txtstream.WriteLine("            If (tstr <> """""") Then")
            txtstream.WriteLine("                tstr = tstr + "","""" ")
            txtstream.WriteLine("            End If")
            txtstream.WriteLine("            tstr = tstr & chr(34) & rs.Fields(x).Value &
chr(34)")
            txtstream.WriteLine("        Next")
            txtstream.WriteLine("        txtstream.Writeline(tstr)")
            txtstream.WriteLine("        tstr = """""" ")
            txtstream.WriteLine("        rs.MoveNext")
            txtstream.WriteLine("    Loop")


        Case "Vertical"

            txtstream.WriteLine("    For x = 0 To rs.Fields.Count - 1")
            txtstream.WriteLine("        tstr = rs.Fields(x).Name")
            txtstream.WriteLine("        rs.MoveFirst()")
            txtstream.WriteLine("        Do While (rs.EOF = False)")
            txtstream.WriteLine("            If (tstr <> """""") Then")
```

```
            txtstream.WriteLine("          tstr = tstr + "","" ")
            txtstream.WriteLine("        End If")
            txtstream.WriteLine("          tstr = tstr & chr(34) & rs.Fields(x).Value &
chr(34)")
            txtstream.WriteLine("        rs.MoveNext")
            txtstream.WriteLine("     Loop")
            txtstream.WriteLine("     txtstream.Writeline(tstr)")
            txtstream.WriteLine("     tstr = """" ")
            txtstream.WriteLine("   Next")



    End Select

    txtstream.WriteLine("")
    txtstream.WriteLine("        txtstream.Close")
    txtstream.WriteLine("")


End Sub


Private Sub Do_Exclamation_Delimited_Code()


    txtstream.WriteLine("   Set ws = CreateObject(""WScript.Shell"")")
    txtstream.WriteLine("   Set fso =
CreateObject(""Scripting.FileSystemObject"")")
    txtstream.WriteLine("   Set txtstream = fso.OpenTextFile(ws.CurrentDirectory +
""\" & Tablename & ".txt""", 2, True, -2)")

    txtstream.WriteLine("   Dim tstr")
    txtstream.WriteLine("   tstr= """" ")

    Select Case Orientation


        Case "Horizontal"


            txtstream.WriteLine("  For x = 0 To rs.Fields.Count - 1")
            txtstream.WriteLine("    If (tstr <> """") Then")
            txtstream.WriteLine("      tstr = tstr + ""!"" ")
            txtstream.WriteLine("    End If")
            txtstream.WriteLine("    tstr = tstr + rs.Fields(x).Name")
            txtstream.WriteLine("  Next")
            txtstream.WriteLine("  txtstream.Writeline(tstr)")
            txtstream.WriteLine("  tstr = """" ")
```

```vb
        txtstream.WriteLine("    rs.MoveFirst()")
        txtstream.WriteLine("    Do While (rs.EOF = False)")
        txtstream.WriteLine("      For x = 0 To rs.Fields.Count - 1")
        txtstream.WriteLine("        If (tstr <> """""") Then")
        txtstream.WriteLine("          tstr = tstr + """!"" ")
        txtstream.WriteLine("        End If")
        txtstream.WriteLine("        tstr = tstr & chr(34) & rs.Fields(x).Value &
chr(34)")
        txtstream.WriteLine("      Next")
        txtstream.WriteLine("      txtstream.Writeline(tstr)")
        txtstream.WriteLine("      tstr = """""" ")
        txtstream.WriteLine("      rs.MoveNext")
        txtstream.WriteLine("    Loop")


      Case "Vertical"


        txtstream.WriteLine("    For x = 0 To rs.Fields.Count - 1")
        txtstream.WriteLine("      tstr = rs.Fields(x).Name")
        txtstream.WriteLine("      rs.MoveFirst()")
        txtstream.WriteLine("      Do While (rs.EOF = False)")
        txtstream.WriteLine("        If (tstr <> """""") Then")
        txtstream.WriteLine("          tstr = tstr + """!"" ")
        txtstream.WriteLine("        End If")
        txtstream.WriteLine("        tstr = tstr & chr(34) & rs.Fields(x).Value &
chr(34)")
        txtstream.WriteLine("        rs.MoveNext")
        txtstream.WriteLine("      Loop")
        txtstream.WriteLine("      txtstream.Writeline(tstr)")
        txtstream.WriteLine("      tstr = """""" ")
        txtstream.WriteLine("    Next")



    End Select

    txtstream.WriteLine("")
    txtstream.WriteLine("      txtstream.Close")
    txtstream.WriteLine("")



  End Sub

  Private Sub Do_Semi_Colon_Delimited_Code()


    txtstream.WriteLine("    Set ws = CreateObject(""WScript.Shell"")")
```

```vb
txtstream.WriteLine("    Set fso = CreateObject(""Scripting.FileSystemObject"")")
txtstream.WriteLine("    Set txtstream = fso.OpenTextFile(ws.CurrentDirectory + ""\"" & Tablename & "".txt"", 2, True, -2)")

txtstream.WriteLine("    Dim tstr")
txtstream.WriteLine("    tstr= """"")

Select Case Orientation

    Case "Horizontal"

        txtstream.WriteLine("    For x = 0 To rs.Fields.Count - 1")
        txtstream.WriteLine("     If (tstr <> """") Then")
        txtstream.WriteLine("       tstr = tstr + "","" ")
        txtstream.WriteLine("     End If")
        txtstream.WriteLine("     tstr = tstr + rs.Fields(x).Name")
        txtstream.WriteLine("    Next")
        txtstream.WriteLine("    txtstream.Writeline(tstr)")
        txtstream.WriteLine("    tstr = """"")
        txtstream.WriteLine("    rs.MoveFirst()")
        txtstream.WriteLine("    Do While (rs.EOF = False)")
        txtstream.WriteLine("     For x = 0 To rs.Fields.Count - 1")
        txtstream.WriteLine("      If (tstr <> """") Then")
        txtstream.WriteLine("        tstr = tstr + "","" ")
        txtstream.WriteLine("      End If")
        txtstream.WriteLine("      tstr = tstr & chr(34) & rs.Fields(x).Value & chr(34)")
        txtstream.WriteLine("     Next")
        txtstream.WriteLine("     txtstream.Writeline(tstr)")
        txtstream.WriteLine("     tstr = """"")
        txtstream.WriteLine("     rs.MoveNext")
        txtstream.WriteLine("    Loop")

    Case "Vertical"

        txtstream.WriteLine("    For x = 0 To rs.Fields.Count - 1")
        txtstream.WriteLine("     tstr = rs.Fields(x).Name")
        txtstream.WriteLine("     rs.MoveFirst()")
        txtstream.WriteLine("     Do While (rs.EOF = False)")
        txtstream.WriteLine("      If (tstr <> """") Then")
        txtstream.WriteLine("        tstr = tstr + "","" ")
        txtstream.WriteLine("      End If")
        txtstream.WriteLine("      tstr = tstr & chr(34) & rs.Fields(x).Value & chr(34)")
        txtstream.WriteLine("      rs.MoveNext")
```

```vba
        txtstream.WriteLine("       Loop")
        txtstream.WriteLine("            txtstream.Writeline(tstr)")
        txtstream.WriteLine("         tstr = """"""" """)
        txtstream.WriteLine("   Next")


    End Select

    txtstream.WriteLine("""")
    txtstream.WriteLine("          txtstream.Close")
    txtstream.WriteLine("""")


End Sub

Private Sub Do_Tab_Delimited_Code()

    txtstream.WriteLine("    Set ws = CreateObject("""WScript.Shell""")")
    txtstream.WriteLine("    Set fso =
CreateObject("""Scripting.FileSystemObject""")")
    txtstream.WriteLine("    Set txtstream = fso.OpenTextFile(ws.CurrentDirectory +
"""\"" & Tablename & "".txt""", 2, True, -2)")

    txtstream.WriteLine("    Dim tstr")
    txtstream.WriteLine("    tstr= """"""" """)

Select Case Orientation


    Case "Horizontal"


        txtstream.WriteLine("    For x = 0 To rs.Fields.Count - 1")
        txtstream.WriteLine("      If (tstr <> """"""") Then")
        txtstream.WriteLine("        tstr = tstr + vbtab ")
        txtstream.WriteLine("      End If")
        txtstream.WriteLine("        tstr = tstr + rs.Fields(x).Name")
        txtstream.WriteLine("    Next")
        txtstream.WriteLine("    txtstream.Writeline(tstr)")
        txtstream.WriteLine("    tstr = """"""" """)
        txtstream.WriteLine("    rs.MoveFirst()")
        txtstream.WriteLine("    Do While (rs.EOF = False)")
        txtstream.WriteLine("      For x = 0 To rs.Fields.Count - 1")
        txtstream.WriteLine("        If (tstr <> """"""") Then")
        txtstream.WriteLine("          tstr = tstr + vbtab ")
        txtstream.WriteLine("        End If")
```

```
            txtstream.WriteLine("            tstr = tstr & chr(34) & rs.Fields(x).Value &
chr(34)")
            txtstream.WriteLine("       Next")
            txtstream.WriteLine("       txtstream.Writeline(tstr)")
            txtstream.WriteLine("       tstr = """" ")
            txtstream.WriteLine("       rs.MoveNext")
            txtstream.WriteLine("   Loop")


        Case "Vertical"


            txtstream.WriteLine("   For x = 0 To rs.Fields.Count - 1")
            txtstream.WriteLine("      tstr = rs.Fields(x).Name")
            txtstream.WriteLine("      rs.MoveFirst()")
            txtstream.WriteLine("      Do While (rs.EOF = False)")
            txtstream.WriteLine("        If (tstr <> """") Then")
            txtstream.WriteLine("          tstr = tstr + vbtab ")
            txtstream.WriteLine("        End If")
            txtstream.WriteLine("          tstr = tstr & chr(34) & rs.Fields(x).Value &
chr(34)")
            txtstream.WriteLine("        rs.MoveNext")
            txtstream.WriteLine("      Loop")
            txtstream.WriteLine("      txtstream.Writeline(tstr)")
            txtstream.WriteLine("      tstr = """" ")
            txtstream.WriteLine("   Next")




    End Select

    txtstream.WriteLine("")
    txtstream.WriteLine("      txtstream.Close")
    txtstream.WriteLine("")



  End Sub

  Private Sub Do_Tilde_Delimited_Code()


    txtstream.WriteLine("   Set ws = CreateObject(""WScript.Shell"")")
    txtstream.WriteLine("   Set fso =
CreateObject(""Scripting.FileSystemObject"")")
    txtstream.WriteLine("   Set txtstream = fso.OpenTextFile(ws.CurrentDirectory +
""\" & Tablename & ".txt""", 2, True, -2)")

    txtstream.WriteLine("   Dim tstr")
```

```vb
txtstream.WriteLine("    tstr= """""" ")

Select Case Orientation

    Case "Horizontal"

            txtstream.WriteLine("    For x = 0 To rs.Fields.Count - 1")
            txtstream.WriteLine("        If (tstr <> """""") Then")
            txtstream.WriteLine("            tstr = tstr + """"~"""" ")
            txtstream.WriteLine("        End If")
            txtstream.WriteLine("        tstr = tstr + rs.Fields(x).Name")
            txtstream.WriteLine("    Next")
            txtstream.WriteLine("    txtstream.Writeline(tstr)")
            txtstream.WriteLine("    tstr = """""" ")
            txtstream.WriteLine("    rs.MoveFirst()")
            txtstream.WriteLine("    Do While (rs.EOF = False)")
            txtstream.WriteLine("        For x = 0 To rs.Fields.Count - 1")
            txtstream.WriteLine("            If (tstr <> """""") Then")
            txtstream.WriteLine("                tstr = tstr + """"~"""" ")
            txtstream.WriteLine("            End If")
            txtstream.WriteLine("            tstr = tstr & chr(34) & rs.Fields(x).Value &
chr(34)")
            txtstream.WriteLine("        Next")
            txtstream.WriteLine("        txtstream.Writeline(tstr)")
            txtstream.WriteLine("        tstr = """""" ")
            txtstream.WriteLine("        rs.MoveNext")
            txtstream.WriteLine("    Loop")


    Case "Vertical"

            txtstream.WriteLine("    For x = 0 To rs.Fields.Count - 1")
            txtstream.WriteLine("        tstr = rs.Fields(x).Name")
            txtstream.WriteLine("        rs.MoveFirst()")
            txtstream.WriteLine("        Do While (rs.EOF = False)")
            txtstream.WriteLine("            If (tstr <> """""") Then")
            txtstream.WriteLine("                tstr = tstr + """"~"""" ")
            txtstream.WriteLine("            End If")
            txtstream.WriteLine("            tstr = tstr & chr(34) & rs.Fields(x).Value &
chr(34)")
            txtstream.WriteLine("            rs.MoveNext")
            txtstream.WriteLine("        Loop")
            txtstream.WriteLine("        txtstream.Writeline(tstr)")
            txtstream.WriteLine("        tstr = """""" ")
            txtstream.WriteLine("    Next")
```

End Select

```
txtstream.WriteLine("")
txtstream.WriteLine("        txtstream.Close")
txtstream.WriteLine("")
```

End Sub

The XML Files

Don't know about you, for some reason everytime I write the XML Files, it sounds like the X Files.

```vbnet
Private Sub Do_Element_XML_Code()
    txtstream.WriteLine("    Set ws = CreateObject("""WScript.Shell""")")
    txtstream.WriteLine("    Set fso =
CreateObject("""Scripting.FileSystemObject""")")
    txtstream.WriteLine("    Set txtstream = fso.OpenTextFile(ws.CurrentDirectory +
"""\" & Tablename & ".txt""", 2, True, -2)")
    txtstream.WriteLine("    txtstream.WriteLine(""<?xml version='1.0'
encoding='iso-8859-1'?>""")")
    txtstream.WriteLine("    txtstream.WriteLine(""<data>""")")
    txtstream.WriteLine("    rs.MoveFirst")
    txtstream.WriteLine("    Do While (rs.EOF = False)")
    txtstream.WriteLine("        txtstream.WriteLine(""<" & Tablename & ">""")")
    txtstream.WriteLine("        For x = 0 To rs.Fields.Count - 1")
    txtstream.WriteLine("            txtstream.WriteLine(""<""" + rs.Fields(x).Name +
""">""" + rs.Fields(x).Value + ""</""" + rs.Fields(x).Name + """>""")")
    txtstream.WriteLine("        Next")
    txtstream.WriteLine("        txtstream.WriteLine(""</" & Tablename & ">""")")
    txtstream.WriteLine("        rs.MoveNext")
    txtstream.WriteLine("    Loop")
    txtstream.WriteLine("    txtstream.WriteLine(""</data>""")")
```

```vb
        txtstream.WriteLine("    txtstream.close()")
        txtstream.WriteLine("")


End Sub

    Private Sub Do_Element_XML_For_XSL_Code()

        txtstream.WriteLine("    Set ws = CreateObject(""WScript.Shell"")")
        txtstream.WriteLine("    Set fso =
CreateObject(""Scripting.FileSystemObject"")")
        txtstream.WriteLine("    Set txtstream = fso.OpenTextFile(ws.CurrentDirectory +
""\"" & Tablename & ".txt""", 2, True, -2)")
        txtstream.WriteLine("    txtstream.WriteLine(""<?xml version='1.0'
encoding='iso-8859-1'?>"")")
        txtstream.WriteLine("    txtstream.WriteLine(""<?xml-stylesheet
type='Text/xsl' href='"" + ws.CurrentDirectory + ""\"" & Tablename & ".xsl""""?>")
        txtstream.WriteLine("    rs.MoveFirst")
        txtstream.WriteLine("    Do While (rs.EOF = False)")
        txtstream.WriteLine("        txtstream.WriteLine(""<"" & Tablename & ">"")")
        txtstream.WriteLine("        For x = 0 To rs.Fields.Count - 1")
        txtstream.WriteLine("            txtstream.WriteLine(""<"" + rs.Fields(x).Name +
"">"" + rs.Fields(x).Value + ""</"" + rs.Fields(x).Name + "">"")")
        txtstream.WriteLine("        Next")
        txtstream.WriteLine("        txtstream.WriteLine(""</"" & Tablename & ">"")")
        txtstream.WriteLine("        rs.MoveNext")
        txtstream.WriteLine("    Loop")
        txtstream.WriteLine("    txtstream.WriteLine(""</data>"")")
        txtstream.WriteLine("    txtstream.close()")
        txtstream.WriteLine("")
        txtstream.WriteLine("    txtstream.close()")


End Sub
```

The Schema XML Code

This routine creates XML and then converts it into the format necessary to create a type of XML that can be used in SRS reports..

Private Sub **Do_Schema_XML_Code()**

```
txtstream.WriteLine("    Set ws = CreateObject(""WScript.Shell"")")
txtstream.WriteLine("    Set fso = CreateObject(""Scripting.FileSystemObject"")")
txtstream.WriteLine("    Set txtstream = fso.OpenTextFile(ws.CurrentDirectory + ""\" & Tablename & ".txt""", 2, True, -2)")
txtstream.WriteLine("    txtstream.WriteLine(""<?xml version='1.0' encoding='iso-8859-1'?>"")")
txtstream.WriteLine("    txtstream.WriteLine(""<data>"")")
txtstream.WriteLine("    rs.MoveFirst")
txtstream.WriteLine("    Do While (rs.EOF = False)")
txtstream.WriteLine("       txtstream.WriteLine(""<" & Tablename & ">"")")
txtstream.WriteLine("       For x = 0 To rs.Fields.Count - 1")
txtstream.WriteLine("          txtstream.WriteLine(""<" + rs.Fields(x).Name + "">"" + rs.Fields(x).Value + ""</" + rs.Fields(x).Name + "">"")")
txtstream.WriteLine("       Next")
txtstream.WriteLine("       txtstream.WriteLine(""</" & Tablename & ">"")")
txtstream.WriteLine("       rs.MoveNext")
txtstream.WriteLine("    Loop")
txtstream.WriteLine("    txtstream.WriteLine(""</data>"")")
txtstream.WriteLine("    txtstream.close()")
txtstream.WriteLine("")
txtstream.WriteLine("    Set rs1 = CreateObject(""ADODB.Recordset"")")
txtstream.WriteLine("    rs1.ActiveConnection = ""Provider=MSDAOSP; Data Source=msxml2.DSOControl"" ")
```

```
    txtstream.WriteLine("    rs1.Open(ws.CurrentDirectory + """\" & Tablename &
".xml""")")
    txtstream.WriteLine("")
    txtstream.WriteLine("    If (fso.FileExists(ws.CurrentDirectory + """\" &
Tablename & "_Schema.xml""") = True) Then")
    txtstream.WriteLine("        fso.DeleteFile(ws.CurrentDirectory + """\" &
Tablename & "_Schema.xml""")")
    txtstream.WriteLine("    End If")
    txtstream.WriteLine("")
    txtstream.WriteLine("    rs.Save(ws.CurrentDirectory + """\" & Tablename &
"_Schema.xml""", 1)")


End Sub
```

The Excel Code

This routine is providing you with both horizontal a vertical views along with doing left alignment of the information and auto sizing columns.

```
Private Sub Do_Excel_Code()

    txtstream.WriteLine("   Set ws = CreateObject(""WScript.Shell"")")
    txtstream.WriteLine("   Set fso =
CreateObject(""Scripting.FileSystemObject"")")
    txtstream.WriteLine("   Set txtstream = fso.OpenTextFile(ws.CurrentDirectory +
""\" & Tablename & ".csv""", 2, True, -2)")

    txtstream.WriteLine("   Dim tstr")
    txtstream.WriteLine("   tstr= """""" ")

Select Case Orientation


    Case "Horizontal"


            txtstream.WriteLine("   For x = 0 To rs.Fields.Count - 1")
            txtstream.WriteLine("     If (tstr <> """""") Then")
            txtstream.WriteLine("       tstr = tstr + "","""" ")
            txtstream.WriteLine("     End If")
            txtstream.WriteLine("     tstr = tstr + rs.Fields(x).Name")
            txtstream.WriteLine("   Next")
            txtstream.WriteLine("   txtstream.Writeline(tstr)")
            txtstream.WriteLine("   tstr = """""" ")
            txtstream.WriteLine("   rs.MoveFirst()")
```

```vb
        txtstream.WriteLine("    Do While (rs.EOF = False)")
        txtstream.WriteLine("      For x = 0 To rs.Fields.Count - 1")
        txtstream.WriteLine("        If (tstr <> """") Then")
        txtstream.WriteLine("          tstr = tstr + "","" ")
        txtstream.WriteLine("        End If")
        txtstream.WriteLine("        tstr = tstr & chr(34) & rs.Fields(x).Value & chr(34)")
        txtstream.WriteLine("      Next")
        txtstream.WriteLine("      txtstream.Writeline(tstr)")
        txtstream.WriteLine("      tstr = """" ")
        txtstream.WriteLine("      rs.MoveNext")
        txtstream.WriteLine("    Loop")

  Case "Vertical"

        txtstream.WriteLine("    For x = 0 To rs.Fields.Count - 1")
        txtstream.WriteLine("      tstr = rs.Fields(x).Name")
        txtstream.WriteLine("      rs.MoveFirst()")
        txtstream.WriteLine("      Do While (rs.EOF = False)")
        txtstream.WriteLine("        If (tstr <> """") Then")
        txtstream.WriteLine("          tstr = tstr + "","" ")
        txtstream.WriteLine("        End If")
        txtstream.WriteLine("        tstr = tstr & chr(34) & rs.Fields(x).Value & chr(34)")
        txtstream.WriteLine("        rs.MoveNext")
        txtstream.WriteLine("      Loop")
        txtstream.WriteLine("      txtstream.Writeline(tstr)")
        txtstream.WriteLine("      tstr = """" ")
        txtstream.WriteLine("    Next")



  End Select

    txtstream.WriteLine("")
    txtstream.WriteLine("    txtstream.Close")
    txtstream.WriteLine("")
    txtstream.WriteLine("    ws.Run(ws.CurrentDirectory + ""\"" & Tablename & "".csv"")")



  End Sub

  Private Sub Do_Excel_Automation_Code()
```

```
Select Case Orientation

    Case "Horizontal"

        txtstream.WriteLine("    Set oExcel = CreateObject(""Excel.Application"")")
        txtstream.WriteLine("    oExcel.Visible = true")
        txtstream.WriteLine("    Set wb = oExcel.Workbooks.Add()")
        txtstream.WriteLine("    Set ws = wb.WorkSheets(1)")
        txtstream.WriteLine("    ws.Name = """" & Tablename & """" ")
        txtstream.WriteLine("    x=1")
        txtstream.WriteLine("    y=2")
        txtstream.WriteLine("    For z = 0 To rs.Fields.Count - 1")
        txtstream.WriteLine("      ws.Cells.Item(1, x) = rs.Fields(z).Name")
        txtstream.WriteLine("      x=x+1")
        txtstream.WriteLine("    Next")
        txtstream.WriteLine("    x=1")
        txtstream.WriteLine("    rs.MoveFirst()")
        txtstream.WriteLine("    Do While rs.EOF = False")
        txtstream.WriteLine("      For z = 0 To rs.Fields.Count - 1")
        txtstream.WriteLine("        ws.Cells.Item(y, x) = rs.Fields(z).Value")
        txtstream.WriteLine("        x=x+1")
        txtstream.WriteLine("      Next")
        txtstream.WriteLine("      x=1")
        txtstream.WriteLine("      y=y+1")
        txtstream.WriteLine("      rs.MoveNext")
        txtstream.WriteLine("    Loop")
        txtstream.WriteLine("")
        txtstream.WriteLine("    ws.Columns.HorizontalAlignment = -4131")
        txtstream.WriteLine("    iret = ws.Columns.AutoFit()")
        txtstream.WriteLine("")

    Case "Vertical"

        txtstream.WriteLine("    Set oExcel = CreateObject(""Excel.Application"")")
        txtstream.WriteLine("    oExcel.Visible = true")
        txtstream.WriteLine("    Set wb = oExcel.Workbooks.Add()")
        txtstream.WriteLine("    Set ws = wb.WorkSheets(1)")
        txtstream.WriteLine("    ws.Name = """" & Tablename & """" ")
        txtstream.WriteLine("    x=1")
        txtstream.WriteLine("    y=2")
        txtstream.WriteLine("    For z = 0 To rs.Fields.Count - 1")
        txtstream.WriteLine("      ws.Cells.Item(x, 1) = rs.Fields(z).Name")
        txtstream.WriteLine("      x=x+1")
        txtstream.WriteLine("    Next")
        txtstream.WriteLine("    x=1")
        txtstream.WriteLine("    rs.MoveFirst()")
        txtstream.WriteLine("    Do While rs.EOF = False")
        txtstream.WriteLine("      For z = 0 To rs.Fields.Count - 1")
        txtstream.WriteLine("        ws.Cells.Item(x, y) = rs.Fields(z).Value")
        txtstream.WriteLine("        x=x+1")
```

```
        txtstream.WriteLine("      Next")
        txtstream.WriteLine("      x=1")
        txtstream.WriteLine("      y=y+1")
        txtstream.WriteLine("      rs.MoveNext")
        txtstream.WriteLine("   Loop")
        txtstream.WriteLine("")
        txtstream.WriteLine("   ws.Columns.HorizontalAlignment = -4131")
        txtstream.WriteLine("   iret = ws.Columns.AutoFit()")
        txtstream.WriteLine("")

    End Select


End Sub
```

The XSL Code

Last but not least is the XSL code and as you will see, the options include table type, orientation and an assortment of controls.

```
Private Sub Write_The_XSL_Code()

    txtstream.WriteLine("    Set ws = CreateObject(""WScript.Shell"")")
    txtstream.WriteLine("    Set fso =
CreateObject(""Scripting.FileSystemObject"")")
    txtstream.WriteLine("    Set txtstream = fso.OpenTextFile(ws.CurrentDirectory +
""\" & Tablename & ".xsl""", 2, true, -2)")
    txtstream.WriteLine("    txtstream.WriteLine(""<?xml version='1.0'
encoding='UTF-8'?>"")")
    txtstream.WriteLine("    txtstream.WriteLine(""<xsl:stylesheet version='1.0'
xmlns:xsl='http://www.w3.org/1999/XSL/Transform'>"")")
    txtstream.WriteLine("    txtstream.WriteLine(""<xsl:template
match=""""""/""""""">"")")
    txtstream.WriteLine("    txtstream.WriteLine(""<html>"")")
    txtstream.WriteLine("    txtstream.WriteLine(""<head>"")")
    txtstream.WriteLine("    txtstream.WriteLine(""<title>Products</title>"")")
    txtstream.WriteLine("    txtstream.WriteLine(""</head>"")")
    Add_StyleSheet()
    txtstream.WriteLine("    txtstream.WriteLine(""<body>"")")
    txtstream.WriteLine("    txtstream.WriteLine(""<table colspacing=""""""3""""""
colpadding=""""""3"""""">"")")
    txtstream.WriteLine("    rs.MoveFirst()")
    txtstream.WriteLine("    ")

    Select Case Orientation
```

Case "Single Line Horizontal"

```
txtstream.WriteLine("    txtstream.WriteLine(""<tr>"")")
txtstream.WriteLine("    for x = 0 to rs.Fields.count-1")
txtstream.WriteLine("        txtstream.WriteLine(""<th align='left'
nowrap='true'>"" + rs.Fields(x).Name + ""</th>"")")
txtstream.WriteLine("    next")
txtstream.WriteLine("    txtstream.WriteLine(""</tr>"")")
txtstream.WriteLine("    txtstream.WriteLine(""<tr>"")")
txtstream.WriteLine("    for x = 0 to rs.Fields.count-1")
```

Select Case ControlType

    Case "None"

```
txtstream.WriteLine("        txtstream.WriteLine(""<td><xsl:value-of
select="""""data/" & Tablename & "/"" + rs.Fields(x).Name + """""/></td>"")")
```

    Case "Button"

```
txtstream.WriteLine("        txtstream.WriteLine(""<td align='left'
nowrap='true'><button style='width:100%;'><xsl:value-of select="""""data/" &
Tablename & "/"" + rs.Fields(x).Name + """""""/></button></td>"")")
```

    Case "Checkbox"

```
txtstream.WriteLine("        txtstream.WriteLine(""<td align='left'
nowrap='true'><input type=Checkbox value="""""" & rs.Fields(x).Value &
""""""></input></td>"")")
```

    Case "Combobox"

```
txtstream.WriteLine("        txtstream.WriteLine(""<td align='left'
nowrap='true'><select><option><xsl:attribute name='value'><xsl:value-of
select="""""data/" & Tablename & "/"" + rs.Fields(x).Name +
"""""""/></xsl:attribute><xsl:value-of select="""""data/" & Tablename & "/"" +
rs.Fields(x).Name + """""""/></option></select></td>"")")
```

    Case "Div"

```
txtstream.WriteLine("        txtstream.WriteLine(""<td align='left'
nowrap='true'><div><xsl:value-of select="""""data/" & Tablename & "/"" +
rs.Fields(x).Name + """""""/></div></td>"")")
```

    Case "Link"

```vb
                    txtstream.WriteLine("            txtstream.WriteLine(""<td  align='left'
nowrap='true'><a href='""" & rs.Fields(x).Value & """'><xsl:value-of
select=""""""data/" & Tablename & "/""" + rs.Fields(x).Name  +
""""""""/></a></td>""")")

            Case "Listbox"

                    txtstream.WriteLine("            txtstream.WriteLine(""<td  align='left'
nowrap='true'><select multiple><option><xsl:attribute name='value'><xsl:value-of
select=""""""data/" & Tablename & "/""" + rs.Fields(x).Name  +
""""""""/></xsl:attribute><xsl:value-of select=""""""data/" & Tablename & "/""" +
rs.Fields(x).Name  + """""""""/></option></select></td>""")")

            Case "Span"

                    txtstream.WriteLine("            txtstream.WriteLine(""<td  align='left'
nowrap='true'><span><xsl:value-of select=""""""data/" & Tablename & "/""" +
rs.Fields(x).Name  + """""""""/></span></td>""")")

            Case "Textarea"

                    txtstream.WriteLine("            txtstream.WriteLine(""<td  align='left'
nowrap='true'><textarea><xsl:value-of select=""""""data/" & Tablename & "/""" +
rs.Fields(x).Name  + """""""""/></textarea></td>""")")

            Case "Textbox"

                    txtstream.WriteLine("            txtstream.WriteLine(""<td  align='left'
nowrap='true'><input type='text'><xsl:attribute name=""""""value"""""">><xsl:value-
of select=""""""data/" & Tablename & "/""" + rs.Fields(x).Name  +
""""""""/></xsl:attribute></input></td>""")")

            End Select


        txtstream.WriteLine("   next ")
        txtstream.WriteLine("   txtstream.WriteLine(""</tr>""")")

    Case "Multi Line Horizontal"

        txtstream.WriteLine("   txtstream.WriteLine(""<tr>""")")
        txtstream.WriteLine("   for x = 0 to rs.Fields.count-1")
        txtstream.WriteLine("      txtstream.WriteLine(""<th>""" +
rs.Fields(x).Name + """</th>""")")
        txtstream.WriteLine("   next")
        txtstream.WriteLine("   txtstream.WriteLine(""</tr>""")")
        txtstream.WriteLine("   txtstream.WriteLine(""<xsl:for-each
select=""""""data/" & Tablename & """""""">""")")
        txtstream.WriteLine("   txtstream.WriteLine(""<tr>""")")
        txtstream.WriteLine("   for x = 0 to rs.Fields.count-1")
```

```
        txtstream.WriteLine("       txtstream.WriteLine(""<td><xsl:value-of
select="""""" "" + rs.Fields(x).Name + "" """"""/></td>"")")

        Select Case ControlType

            Case "None"

                txtstream.WriteLine("       txtstream.WriteLine(""<td><xsl:value-of
select="""""""" + rs.Fields(x).Name + """"""""/></td>"")")

            Case "Button"

                txtstream.WriteLine("       txtstream.WriteLine(""<td  align='left'
nowrap='true'><button style='width:100%;'><xsl:value-of select="""""""" +
rs.Fields(x).Name + """"""""/></button></td>"")")

            Case "Combobox"

                txtstream.WriteLine("       txtstream.WriteLine(""<td  align='left'
nowrap='true'><select><option><xsl:attribute name='value'><xsl:value-of
select="""""""" + rs.Fields(x).Name + """"""""/></xsl:attribute><xsl:value-of
select=""""""data/" & Tablename & "/"""" + rs.Fields(x).Name +
""""""""/></option></select></td>"")")

            Case "Div"

                txtstream.WriteLine("       txtstream.WriteLine(""<td  align='left'
nowrap='true'><div><xsl:value-of select=""""""data/" & Tablename & "/"""" +
rs.Fields(x).Name + """"""""/></div></td>"")")

            Case "Link"

                txtstream.WriteLine("       txtstream.WriteLine(""<td  align='left'
nowrap='true'><a href='""" & rs.Fields(x).Value & ""'><xsl:value-of
select=""""""data/" & Tablename & "/"""" + rs.Fields(x).Name +
""""""""/></a></td>"")")

            Case "Listbox"

                txtstream.WriteLine("       txtstream.WriteLine(""<td  align='left'
nowrap='true'><select multiple><option><xsl:attribute name='value'><xsl:value-of
select=""""""data/" & Tablename & "/"""" + rs.Fields(x).Name +
""""""""/></xsl:attribute><xsl:value-of select=""""""data/" & Tablename & "/"""" +
rs.Fields(x).Name + """"""""/></option></select></td>"")")

            Case "Span"
```

```vb
                txtstream.WriteLine("        txtstream.WriteLine(""<td align='left'
nowrap='true'><span><xsl:value-of select="""""data/" & Tablename & "/""" +
rs.Fields(x).Name + """"""""/></span></td>"")")

        Case "Textarea"

                txtstream.WriteLine("        txtstream.WriteLine(""<td align='left'
nowrap='true'><textarea><xsl:value-of select="""""data/" & Tablename & "/""" +
rs.Fields(x).Name + """""""""/></textarea></td>"")")

        Case "Textbox"

                txtstream.WriteLine("        txtstream.WriteLine(""<td align='left'
nowrap='true'><input type='text'><xsl:attribute name="""""value"""""><xsl:value-
of select="""""data/" & Tablename & "/""" + rs.Fields(x).Name +
"""""""""/></xsl:attribute></input></td>"")")

        End Select

        txtstream.WriteLine("    next")
        txtstream.WriteLine("    txtstream.WriteLine(""</tr>"")")
        txtstream.WriteLine("    txtstream.WriteLine(""</xsl:for-each>"")")

    Case "Single Line Vertical"

        txtstream.WriteLine("    for x = 0 to rs.Fields.count-1")
        txtstream.WriteLine("        txtstream.WriteLine(""<tr><th>"" +
rs.Fields(x).Name + ""</th>"")")

        Select Case ControlType

            Case "None"

                txtstream.WriteLine("        txtstream.WriteLine(""<td><xsl:value-of
select="""""data/" & Tablename & "/""" + rs.Fields(x).Name +
"""""""""/></td></tr>"")")

            Case "Button"

                txtstream.WriteLine("        txtstream.WriteLine(""<td align='left'
nowrap='true'><button style='width:100%;'><xsl:value-of select="""""data/" &
Tablename & "/""" + rs.Fields(x).Name + """"""""/></button></td></tr>"")")

            Case "Checkbox"

                txtstream.WriteLine("        txtstream.WriteLine(""<td align='left'
nowrap='true'><input type=Checkbox value="""""""" & rs.Fields(x).Value &
""""""""></input></td></tr>"")")

            Case "Combobox"
```

```vb
            txtstream.WriteLine("            txtstream.WriteLine(""""<td align='left'
nowrap='true'><select><option><xsl:attribute name='value'><xsl:value-of
select="""""""data/" & Tablename & "/"" + rs.Fields(x).Name +
"""""""""/></xsl:attribute><xsl:value-of select="""""""data/" & Tablename & "/"" +
rs.Fields(x).Name + """"""""""/></option></select></td></tr>"""")")

        Case "Div"

            txtstream.WriteLine("            txtstream.WriteLine(""""<td align='left'
nowrap='true'><div><xsl:value-of select="""""""data/" & Tablename & "/"" +
rs.Fields(x).Name + """""""""/></div></td></tr>"""")")

        Case "Link"

            txtstream.WriteLine("            txtstream.WriteLine(""""<td align='left'
nowrap='true'><a href='"" & rs.Fields(x).Value & """"><xsl:value-of
select="""""""data/" & Tablename & "/"" + rs.Fields(x).Name +
"""""""""/></a></td></tr>"""")")

        Case "Listbox"

            txtstream.WriteLine("            txtstream.WriteLine(""""<td align='left'
nowrap='true'><select multiple><option><xsl:attribute name='value'><xsl:value-of
select="""""""data/" & Tablename & "/"" + rs.Fields(x).Name +
"""""""""/></xsl:attribute><xsl:value-of select="""""""data/" & Tablename & "/"" +
rs.Fields(x).Name + """"""""""/></option></select></td></tr>"""")")

        Case "Span"

            txtstream.WriteLine("            txtstream.WriteLine(""""<td align='left'
nowrap='true'><span><xsl:value-of select="""""""data/" & Tablename & "/"" +
rs.Fields(x).Name + """""""""/></span></td></tr>"""")")

        Case "Textarea"

            txtstream.WriteLine("            txtstream.WriteLine(""""<td align='left'
nowrap='true'><textarea><xsl:value-of select="""""""data/" & Tablename & "/"" +
rs.Fields(x).Name + """""""""/></textarea></td></tr>"""")")

        Case "Textbox"

            txtstream.WriteLine("            txtstream.WriteLine(""""<td align='left'
nowrap='true'><input type='text'><xsl:attribute name="""""""value"""""""><xsl:value-
of select="""""""data/" & Tablename & "/"" + rs.Fields(x).Name +
"""""""""/></xsl:attribute></input></td></tr>"""")")

        End Select
```

```vb
txtstream.WriteLine("    next")

Case "Multi Line Vertical"


txtstream.WriteLine("    for x = 0 to rs.Fields.count-1")
txtstream.WriteLine("        txtstream.WriteLine(""<tr><th align='left'
nowrap='true'>"" + rs.Fields(x).Name + ""</th>"")")



Select Case ControlType

    Case "None"

            txtstream.WriteLine("        txtstream.WriteLine(""<xsl:for-each
select="""""data/" & Tablename & """"""><td align='left' nowrap='true'><xsl:value-
of select="""""" + rs.Fields(x).Name + """"""/></td></xsl:for-each></tr>"")")


    Case "Button"

            txtstream.WriteLine("           txtstream.WriteLine(""<xsl:for-each
select="""""data/" & Tablename & """"""><td align='left' nowrap='true'><button
style='width:100%;'><xsl:value-of select="""""" + rs.Fields(x).Name  +
""""""/></button></td></xsl:for-each></tr>"")")


    Case "Combobox"

            txtstream.WriteLine("        txtstream.WriteLine(""<xsl:for-each
select="""""data/" & Tablename & """"""><td align='left'
nowrap='true'><select><option><xsl:attribute name='value'><xsl:value-of
select="""""" + rs.Fields(x).Name  + """"""/></xsl:attribute><xsl:value-of
select="""""data/" & Tablename & "/"" + rs.Fields(x).Name +
""""""/></option></select></td></xsl:for-each></tr>"")")


    Case "Div"

            txtstream.WriteLine("        txtstream.WriteLine(""<xsl:for-each
select="""""data/" & Tablename & """"""><td  align='left'
nowrap='true'><div><xsl:value-of select="""""data/" & Tablename & "/"" +
rs.Fields(x).Name + """"""/></div></td></xsl:for-each></tr>"")")


    Case "Link"

            txtstream.WriteLine("        txtstream.WriteLine(""<xsl:for-each
select="""""data/" & Tablename & """"""><td  align='left' nowrap='true'><a
href='"" & rs.Fields(x).Value & ""'><xsl:value-of select="""""data/" & Tablename &
"/"" + rs.Fields(x).Name  + """"""/></a></td></xsl:for-each></tr>"")")

    Case "Listbox"
```

```vb
                txtstream.WriteLine("        txtstream.WriteLine(""<xsl:for-each
select="""""data/" & Tablename & """"""><td align='left' nowrap='true'><select
multiple><option><xsl:attribute name='value'><xsl:value-of select="""""data/" &
Tablename & "/""" + rs.Fields(x).Name + """"""""/></xsl:attribute><xsl:value-of
select="""""data/" & Tablename & "/""" + rs.Fields(x).Name +
""""""""/></option></select></td></xsl:for-each></tr>"")")

        Case "Span"

                txtstream.WriteLine("        txtstream.WriteLine(""<xsl:for-each
select="""""data/" & Tablename & """"""><td align='left'
nowrap='true'><span><xsl:value-of select="""""data/" & Tablename & "/""" +
rs.Fields(x).Name + """"""""/></span></td></xsl:for-each></tr>"")")

        Case "Textarea"

                txtstream.WriteLine("        txtstream.WriteLine(""<xsl:for-each
select="""""data/" & Tablename & """"""><td align='left'
nowrap='true'><textarea><xsl:value-of select="""""data/" & Tablename & "/""" +
rs.Fields(x).Name + """"""""/></textarea></td></xsl:for-each></tr>"")")

        Case "Textbox"

                txtstream.WriteLine("        txtstream.WriteLine(""<xsl:for-each
select="""""data/" & Tablename & """"""><td align='left' nowrap='true'><input
type='text'><xsl:attribute name="""""value"""""><xsl:value-of select="""""data/" &
Tablename & "/""" + rs.Fields(x).Name +
""""""""/></xsl:attribute></input></td></xsl:for-each></tr>"")")

        End Select

        txtstream.WriteLine("    next")

    End Select

End Sub
```

The Stylesheet section

Below, is the stylesheet section. You can add some additional stylesheets or use none of them.

```
Private Sub Add_StyleSheet()

    Select Case StyleSheet

        Case "RAW", "raw"

        Case "In Line"

        Case "None"

            txtstream.WriteLine("   txtstream.WriteLine(""""<style type='text/css'>"""")")
            txtstream.WriteLine("   txtstream.WriteLine(""""th"""")")
            txtstream.WriteLine("   txtstream.WriteLine(""""{"""")")
            txtstream.WriteLine("   txtstream.WriteLine(""""   COLOR: white;"""")")
            txtstream.WriteLine("   txtstream.WriteLine(""""}"""")")
            txtstream.WriteLine("   txtstream.WriteLine(""""td"""")")
            txtstream.WriteLine("   txtstream.WriteLine(""""{"""")")
            txtstream.WriteLine("   txtstream.WriteLine(""""   COLOR: white;"""")")
            txtstream.WriteLine("   txtstream.WriteLine(""""}"""")")
            txtstream.WriteLine("   txtstream.WriteLine(""""</style>"""")")

        Case "Its A Table"
```

```
        txtstream.WriteLine("    txtstream.WriteLine(""<style
type='text/css'>"")")
        txtstream.WriteLine("    txtstream.WriteLine(""#itsthetable {"")")
        txtstream.WriteLine("    txtstream.WriteLine(""    font-family: Georgia,
""""Times New Roman"""", Times, serif;"")")
        txtstream.WriteLine("    txtstream.WriteLine(""    color: #036;"")")
        txtstream.WriteLine("    txtstream.WriteLine(""}"")")

        txtstream.WriteLine("    txtstream.WriteLine(""caption {"")")
        txtstream.WriteLine("    txtstream.WriteLine(""    font-size: 48px;"")")
        txtstream.WriteLine("    txtstream.WriteLine(""    color: #036;"")")
        txtstream.WriteLine("    txtstream.WriteLine(""    font-weight:
bolder;"")")
        txtstream.WriteLine("    txtstream.WriteLine(""    font-variant: small-
caps;"")")
        txtstream.WriteLine("    txtstream.WriteLine(""}"")")

        txtstream.WriteLine("    txtstream.WriteLine(""th {"")")
        txtstream.WriteLine("    txtstream.WriteLine(""    font-size: 12px;"")")
        txtstream.WriteLine("    txtstream.WriteLine(""    color: #FFF;"")")
        txtstream.WriteLine("    txtstream.WriteLine(""    background-color:
#06C;"")")
        txtstream.WriteLine("    txtstream.WriteLine(""    padding: 8px
4px;"")")
        txtstream.WriteLine("    txtstream.WriteLine(""    border-bottom: 1px
solid #015ebc;"")")
        txtstream.WriteLine("    txtstream.WriteLine(""}"")")

        txtstream.WriteLine("    txtstream.WriteLine(""table {"")")
        txtstream.WriteLine("    txtstream.WriteLine(""    margin: 0;"")")
        txtstream.WriteLine("    txtstream.WriteLine(""    padding: 0;"")")
        txtstream.WriteLine("    txtstream.WriteLine(""    border-collapse:
collapse;"")")
        txtstream.WriteLine("    txtstream.WriteLine(""    border: 1px solid
#06C;"")")
        txtstream.WriteLine("    txtstream.WriteLine(""    width: 100%"")")
        txtstream.WriteLine("    txtstream.WriteLine(""}"")")

        txtstream.WriteLine("    txtstream.WriteLine(""#itsthetable th a:link,
#itsthetable th a:visited {"")")
        txtstream.WriteLine("    txtstream.WriteLine(""    color: #FFF;"")")
        txtstream.WriteLine("    txtstream.WriteLine(""    text-decoration:
none;"")")
        txtstream.WriteLine("    txtstream.WriteLine(""    border-left: 5px solid
#FFF;"")")
        txtstream.WriteLine("    txtstream.WriteLine(""    padding-left:
3px;"")")
        txtstream.WriteLine("    txtstream.WriteLine(""}"")")
```

```
        txtstream.WriteLine("    txtstream.WriteLine("""th a:hover, #itsthetable th
a:active {""")")
        txtstream.WriteLine("    txtstream.WriteLine("""        color: #F90;""")")
        txtstream.WriteLine("    txtstream.WriteLine("""        text-decoration: line-
through;""")")
        txtstream.WriteLine("    txtstream.WriteLine("""        border-left: 5px solid
#F90;""")")
        txtstream.WriteLine("    txtstream.WriteLine("""        padding-left:
3px;""")")
        txtstream.WriteLine("    txtstream.WriteLine("""}""")")

        txtstream.WriteLine("    txtstream.WriteLine("""tbody th:hover {""")")
        txtstream.WriteLine("    txtstream.WriteLine("""        background-image:
url(imgs/tbody_hover.gif);""")")
        txtstream.WriteLine("    txtstream.WriteLine("""        background-position:
bottom;""")")
        txtstream.WriteLine("    txtstream.WriteLine("""        background-repeat:
repeat-x;""")")
        txtstream.WriteLine("    txtstream.WriteLine("""}""")")

        txtstream.WriteLine("    txtstream.WriteLine("""td {""")")
        txtstream.WriteLine("    txtstream.WriteLine("""        background-color:
#f2f2f2;""")")
        txtstream.WriteLine("    txtstream.WriteLine("""        padding: 4px;""")")
        txtstream.WriteLine("    txtstream.WriteLine("""        font-size: 12px;""")")
        txtstream.WriteLine("    txtstream.WriteLine("""}""")")

        txtstream.WriteLine("    txtstream.WriteLine("""#itsthetable td:hover
{""")")
        txtstream.WriteLine("    txtstream.WriteLine("""        background-color:
#f8f8f8;""")")

        txtstream.WriteLine("    txtstream.WriteLine("""}""")")

        txtstream.WriteLine("    txtstream.WriteLine("""#itsthetable td a:link,
#itsthetable td a:visited {""")")
        txtstream.WriteLine("    txtstream.WriteLine("""        color: #039;""")")
        txtstream.WriteLine("    txtstream.WriteLine("""        text-decoration:
none;""")")
        txtstream.WriteLine("    txtstream.WriteLine("""        border-left: 3px solid
#039;""")")
        txtstream.WriteLine("    txtstream.WriteLine("""        padding-left:
3px;""")")
        txtstream.WriteLine("    txtstream.WriteLine("""}""")")

        txtstream.WriteLine("    txtstream.WriteLine("""#itsthetable td a:hover,
#itsthetable td a:active {""")")
        txtstream.WriteLine("    txtstream.WriteLine("""        color: #06C;""")")
        txtstream.WriteLine("    txtstream.WriteLine("""        text-decoration: line-
through;""")")
```

```
        txtstream.WriteLine("    txtstream.WriteLine(""        border-left: 3px solid
#06C;"")")
        txtstream.WriteLine("    txtstream.WriteLine(""        padding-left:
3px;"")")
        txtstream.WriteLine("    txtstream.WriteLine(""}"")")

        txtstream.WriteLine("    txtstream.WriteLine(""#itsthetable th {"")")
        txtstream.WriteLine("    txtstream.WriteLine(""        text-align: left;"")")
        txtstream.WriteLine("    txtstream.WriteLine(""        width: 150px;"")")
        txtstream.WriteLine("    txtstream.WriteLine(""}"")")

        txtstream.WriteLine("    txtstream.WriteLine(""#itsthetable tr {"")")
        txtstream.WriteLine("    txtstream.WriteLine(""        border-bottom: 1px
solid #CCC;"")")
        txtstream.WriteLine("    txtstream.WriteLine(""}"")")

        txtstream.WriteLine("    txtstream.WriteLine(""#itsthetable thead th
{"")")
        txtstream.WriteLine("    txtstream.WriteLine(""        background-image:
url(imgs/thead_back.gif);"")")
        txtstream.WriteLine("    txtstream.WriteLine(""        background-repeat:
repeat-x;"")")
        txtstream.WriteLine("    txtstream.WriteLine(""        background-color:
#06C;"")")
        txtstream.WriteLine("    txtstream.WriteLine(""        height: 30px;"")")
        txtstream.WriteLine("    txtstream.WriteLine(""        font-size: 18px;"")")
        txtstream.WriteLine("    txtstream.WriteLine(""        text-align:
center;"")")
        txtstream.WriteLine("    txtstream.WriteLine(""        text-shadow: #333
2px 2px;"")")
        txtstream.WriteLine("    txtstream.WriteLine(""        border: 2px;"")")
        txtstream.WriteLine("    txtstream.WriteLine(""}"")")

        txtstream.WriteLine("    txtstream.WriteLine(""#itsthetable tfoot th {"")")
        txtstream.WriteLine("    txtstream.WriteLine(""        background-image:
url(imgs/tfoot_back.gif);"")")
        txtstream.WriteLine("    txtstream.WriteLine(""        background-repeat:
repeat-x;"")")
        txtstream.WriteLine("    txtstream.WriteLine(""        background-color:
#036;"")")
        txtstream.WriteLine("    txtstream.WriteLine(""        height: 30px;"")")
        txtstream.WriteLine("    txtstream.WriteLine(""        font-size: 28px;"")")
        txtstream.WriteLine("    txtstream.WriteLine(""        text-align:
center;"")")
        txtstream.WriteLine("    txtstream.WriteLine(""        text-shadow: #333
2px 2px;"")")
        txtstream.WriteLine("    txtstream.WriteLine(""}"")")

        txtstream.WriteLine("    txtstream.WriteLine(""#itsthetable tfoot td {"")")
```

```
            txtstream.WriteLine("    txtstream.WriteLine(""        background-image:
url(imgs/tfoot_back.gif);"")")
            txtstream.WriteLine("    txtstream.WriteLine(""        background-repeat:
repeat-x;"")")
            txtstream.WriteLine("    txtstream.WriteLine(""        background-color:
#036;"")")
            txtstream.WriteLine("    txtstream.WriteLine(""        color: FFF;"")")
            txtstream.WriteLine("    txtstream.WriteLine(""        height: 30px;"")")
            txtstream.WriteLine("    txtstream.WriteLine(""        font-size: 24px;"")")
            txtstream.WriteLine("    txtstream.WriteLine(""        text-align: left;"")")
            txtstream.WriteLine("    txtstream.WriteLine(""        text-shadow: #333
2px 2px;"")")
            txtstream.WriteLine("    txtstream.WriteLine(""}"")")

            txtstream.WriteLine("    txtstream.WriteLine(""tbody td
a[href="""""http://www.csslab.cl/"""""] {"")")
            txtstream.WriteLine("    txtstream.WriteLine(""        font-weight:
bolder;"")")
            txtstream.WriteLine("    txtstream.WriteLine(""}"")")
            txtstream.WriteLine("    txtstream.WriteLine(""</style>"")")


        Case "Black and White Text"

            txtstream.WriteLine("    txtstream.WriteLine(""<style
type='text/css'>"")")
            txtstream.WriteLine("    txtstream.WriteLine(""th"")")
            txtstream.WriteLine("    txtstream.WriteLine(""{"")")
            txtstream.WriteLine("    txtstream.WriteLine(""    COLOR: white;"")")
            txtstream.WriteLine("    txtstream.WriteLine(""    BACKGROUND-COLOR:
black;"")")
            txtstream.WriteLine("    txtstream.WriteLine(""    FONT-FAMILY:font-
family: Cambria, serif;"")")
            txtstream.WriteLine("    txtstream.WriteLine(""    FONT-SIZE: 12px;"")")
            txtstream.WriteLine("    txtstream.WriteLine(""    text-align: left;"")")
            txtstream.WriteLine("    txtstream.WriteLine(""    white-Space:
nowrap='nowrap';"")")
            txtstream.WriteLine("    txtstream.WriteLine(""}"")")
            txtstream.WriteLine("    txtstream.WriteLine(""td"")")
            txtstream.WriteLine("    txtstream.WriteLine(""{"")")
            txtstream.WriteLine("    txtstream.WriteLine(""    COLOR: white;"")")
            txtstream.WriteLine("    txtstream.WriteLine(""    BACKGROUND-COLOR:
black;"")")
            txtstream.WriteLine("    txtstream.WriteLine(""    FONT-FAMILY: font-
family: Cambria, serif;"")")
            txtstream.WriteLine("    txtstream.WriteLine(""    FONT-SIZE: 12px;"")")
            txtstream.WriteLine("    txtstream.WriteLine(""    text-align: left;"")")
            txtstream.WriteLine("    txtstream.WriteLine(""    white-Space:
nowrap='nowrap';"")")
            txtstream.WriteLine("    txtstream.WriteLine(""}"")")
```

```
txtstream.WriteLine("    txtstream.WriteLine("""div""")")
txtstream.WriteLine("    txtstream.WriteLine("""{""")")
txtstream.WriteLine("    txtstream.WriteLine("""   COLOR: white;""")")
txtstream.WriteLine("    txtstream.WriteLine("""   BACKGROUND-COLOR: black;""")")
txtstream.WriteLine("    txtstream.WriteLine("""   FONT-FAMILY: font-family: Cambria, serif;""")")
txtstream.WriteLine("    txtstream.WriteLine("""   FONT-SIZE: 10px;""")")
txtstream.WriteLine("    txtstream.WriteLine("""   text-align: left;""")")
txtstream.WriteLine("    txtstream.WriteLine("""   white-Space: nowrap='nowrap';""")")
txtstream.WriteLine("    txtstream.WriteLine("""}""")")
txtstream.WriteLine("    txtstream.WriteLine("""span""")")
txtstream.WriteLine("    txtstream.WriteLine("""{""")")
txtstream.WriteLine("    txtstream.WriteLine("""   COLOR: white;""")")
txtstream.WriteLine("    txtstream.WriteLine("""   BACKGROUND-COLOR: black;""")")
txtstream.WriteLine("    txtstream.WriteLine("""   FONT-FAMILY: font-family: Cambria, serif;""")")
txtstream.WriteLine("    txtstream.WriteLine("""   FONT-SIZE: 10px;""")")
txtstream.WriteLine("    txtstream.WriteLine("""   text-align: left;""")")
txtstream.WriteLine("    txtstream.WriteLine("""   white-Space: nowrap='nowrap';""")")
txtstream.WriteLine("    txtstream.WriteLine("""   display:inline-block;""")")
txtstream.WriteLine("    txtstream.WriteLine("""   width: 100%;""")")
txtstream.WriteLine("    txtstream.WriteLine("""}""")")
txtstream.WriteLine("    txtstream.WriteLine("""textarea""")")
txtstream.WriteLine("    txtstream.WriteLine("""{""")")
txtstream.WriteLine("    txtstream.WriteLine("""   COLOR: white;""")")
txtstream.WriteLine("    txtstream.WriteLine("""   BACKGROUND-COLOR: black;""")")
txtstream.WriteLine("    txtstream.WriteLine("""   FONT-FAMILY: font-family: Cambria, serif;""")")
txtstream.WriteLine("    txtstream.WriteLine("""   FONT-SIZE: 10px;""")")
txtstream.WriteLine("    txtstream.WriteLine("""   text-align: left;""")")
txtstream.WriteLine("    txtstream.WriteLine("""   white-Space: nowrap='nowrap';""")")
txtstream.WriteLine("    txtstream.WriteLine("""   width: 100%;""")")
txtstream.WriteLine("    txtstream.WriteLine("""}""")")
txtstream.WriteLine("    txtstream.WriteLine("""select""")")
txtstream.WriteLine("    txtstream.WriteLine("""{""")")
txtstream.WriteLine("    txtstream.WriteLine("""   COLOR: white;""")")
txtstream.WriteLine("    txtstream.WriteLine("""   BACKGROUND-COLOR: black;""")")
txtstream.WriteLine("    txtstream.WriteLine("""   FONT-FAMILY: font-family: Cambria, serif;""")")
txtstream.WriteLine("    txtstream.WriteLine("""   FONT-SIZE: 10px;""")")
txtstream.WriteLine("    txtstream.WriteLine("""   text-align: left;""")")
```

```
        txtstream.WriteLine("    txtstream.WriteLine(""    white-Space:
nowrap='nowrap';"")")
        txtstream.WriteLine("    txtstream.WriteLine(""    width: 100%;"")")
        txtstream.WriteLine("    txtstream.WriteLine(""}"")")
        txtstream.WriteLine("    txtstream.WriteLine(""input"")")
        txtstream.WriteLine("    txtstream.WriteLine(""{"")")
        txtstream.WriteLine("    txtstream.WriteLine(""    COLOR: white;"")")
        txtstream.WriteLine("    txtstream.WriteLine(""    BACKGROUND-COLOR:
black;"")")
        txtstream.WriteLine("    txtstream.WriteLine(""    FONT-FAMILY: font-
family: Cambria, serif;"")")
        txtstream.WriteLine("    txtstream.WriteLine(""    FONT-SIZE: 12px;"")")
        txtstream.WriteLine("    txtstream.WriteLine(""    text-align: left;"")")
        txtstream.WriteLine("    txtstream.WriteLine(""    display:table-cell;"")")
        txtstream.WriteLine("    txtstream.WriteLine(""    white-Space:
nowrap='nowrap';"")")
        txtstream.WriteLine("    txtstream.WriteLine(""}"")")
        txtstream.WriteLine("    txtstream.WriteLine(""h1 {"")")
        txtstream.WriteLine("    txtstream.WriteLine(""color: antiquewhite;"")")
        txtstream.WriteLine("    txtstream.WriteLine(""text-shadow: 1px 1px 1px
black;"")")
        txtstream.WriteLine("    txtstream.WriteLine(""padding: 3px;"")")
        txtstream.WriteLine("    txtstream.WriteLine(""text-align: center;"")")
        txtstream.WriteLine("    txtstream.WriteLine(""box-shadow: inset 2px 2px
5px rgba(0,0,0,0.5), inset -2px -2px 5px rgba(255,255,255,0.5);"")")
        txtstream.WriteLine("    txtstream.WriteLine(""}"")")
        txtstream.WriteLine("    txtstream.WriteLine(""</style>"")")

        Case "Colored Text"


        txtstream.WriteLine("    txtstream.WriteLine(""<style
type='text/css'>"")")
        txtstream.WriteLine("    txtstream.WriteLine(""th"")")
        txtstream.WriteLine("    txtstream.WriteLine(""{"")")
        txtstream.WriteLine("    txtstream.WriteLine(""    COLOR: darkred;"")")
        txtstream.WriteLine("    txtstream.WriteLine(""    BACKGROUND-COLOR:
#eeeeee;"")")
        txtstream.WriteLine("    txtstream.WriteLine(""    FONT-FAMILY:font-
family: Cambria, serif;"")")
        txtstream.WriteLine("    txtstream.WriteLine(""    FONT-SIZE: 12px;"")")
        txtstream.WriteLine("    txtstream.WriteLine(""    text-align: left;"")")
        txtstream.WriteLine("    txtstream.WriteLine(""    white-Space:
nowrap='nowrap';"")")
        txtstream.WriteLine("    txtstream.WriteLine(""}"")")
        txtstream.WriteLine("    txtstream.WriteLine(""td"")")
        txtstream.WriteLine("    txtstream.WriteLine(""{"")")
        txtstream.WriteLine("    txtstream.WriteLine(""    COLOR: navy;"")")
        txtstream.WriteLine("    txtstream.WriteLine(""    BACKGROUND-COLOR:
#eeeeee;"")")
```

```
        txtstream.WriteLine("    txtstream.WriteLine(""   FONT-FAMILY: font-
family: Cambria, serif;"")")
        txtstream.WriteLine("    txtstream.WriteLine(""   FONT-SIZE: 12px;"")")
        txtstream.WriteLine("    txtstream.WriteLine(""   text-align: left;"")")
        txtstream.WriteLine("    txtstream.WriteLine(""   white-Space:
nowrap='nowrap';"")")
        txtstream.WriteLine("    txtstream.WriteLine(""}"")")
        txtstream.WriteLine("    txtstream.WriteLine(""div"")")
        txtstream.WriteLine("    txtstream.WriteLine(""{"")")
        txtstream.WriteLine("    txtstream.WriteLine(""   COLOR: white;"")")
        txtstream.WriteLine("    txtstream.WriteLine(""   BACKGROUND-COLOR:
navy;"")")
        txtstream.WriteLine("    txtstream.WriteLine(""   FONT-FAMILY: font-
family: Cambria, serif;"")")
        txtstream.WriteLine("    txtstream.WriteLine(""   FONT-SIZE: 10px;"")")
        txtstream.WriteLine("    txtstream.WriteLine(""   text-align: left;"")")
        txtstream.WriteLine("    txtstream.WriteLine(""   white-Space:
nowrap='nowrap';"")")
        txtstream.WriteLine("    txtstream.WriteLine(""}"")")
        txtstream.WriteLine("    txtstream.WriteLine(""span"")")
        txtstream.WriteLine("    txtstream.WriteLine(""{"")")
        txtstream.WriteLine("    txtstream.WriteLine(""   COLOR: white;"")")
        txtstream.WriteLine("    txtstream.WriteLine(""   BACKGROUND-COLOR:
navy;"")")
        txtstream.WriteLine("    txtstream.WriteLine(""   FONT-FAMILY: font-
family: Cambria, serif;"")")
        txtstream.WriteLine("    txtstream.WriteLine(""   FONT-SIZE: 10px;"")")
        txtstream.WriteLine("    txtstream.WriteLine(""   text-align: left;"")")
        txtstream.WriteLine("    txtstream.WriteLine(""   white-Space:
nowrap='nowrap';"")")
        txtstream.WriteLine("    txtstream.WriteLine(""   display:inline-
block;"")")
        txtstream.WriteLine("    txtstream.WriteLine(""   width: 100%;"")")
        txtstream.WriteLine("    txtstream.WriteLine(""}"")")
        txtstream.WriteLine("    txtstream.WriteLine(""textarea"")")
        txtstream.WriteLine("    txtstream.WriteLine(""{"")")
        txtstream.WriteLine("    txtstream.WriteLine(""   COLOR: white;"")")
        txtstream.WriteLine("    txtstream.WriteLine(""   BACKGROUND-COLOR:
navy;"")")
        txtstream.WriteLine("    txtstream.WriteLine(""   FONT-FAMILY: font-
family: Cambria, serif;"")")
        txtstream.WriteLine("    txtstream.WriteLine(""   FONT-SIZE: 10px;"")")
        txtstream.WriteLine("    txtstream.WriteLine(""   text-align: left;"")")
        txtstream.WriteLine("    txtstream.WriteLine(""   white-Space:
nowrap='nowrap';"")")
        txtstream.WriteLine("    txtstream.WriteLine(""   width: 100%;"")")
        txtstream.WriteLine("    txtstream.WriteLine(""}"")")
        txtstream.WriteLine("    txtstream.WriteLine(""select"")")
        txtstream.WriteLine("    txtstream.WriteLine(""{"")")
        txtstream.WriteLine("    txtstream.WriteLine(""   COLOR: white;"")")
```

```vb
        txtstream.WriteLine("    txtstream.WriteLine(""    BACKGROUND-COLOR: navy;"")")
        txtstream.WriteLine("    txtstream.WriteLine(""    FONT-FAMILY: font-family: Cambria, serif;"")")
        txtstream.WriteLine("    txtstream.WriteLine(""    FONT-SIZE: 10px;"")")
        txtstream.WriteLine("    txtstream.WriteLine(""    text-align: left;"")")
        txtstream.WriteLine("    txtstream.WriteLine(""    white-Space: nowrap='nowrap';"")")
        txtstream.WriteLine("    txtstream.WriteLine(""    width: 100%;"")")
        txtstream.WriteLine("    txtstream.WriteLine(""}"")")
        txtstream.WriteLine("    txtstream.WriteLine(""input"")")
        txtstream.WriteLine("    txtstream.WriteLine(""{"")")
        txtstream.WriteLine("    txtstream.WriteLine(""    COLOR: white;"")")
        txtstream.WriteLine("    txtstream.WriteLine(""    BACKGROUND-COLOR: navy;"")")
        txtstream.WriteLine("    txtstream.WriteLine(""    FONT-FAMILY: font-family: Cambria, serif;"")")
        txtstream.WriteLine("    txtstream.WriteLine(""    FONT-SIZE: 12px;"")")
        txtstream.WriteLine("    txtstream.WriteLine(""    text-align: left;"")")
        txtstream.WriteLine("    txtstream.WriteLine(""    display:table-cell;"")")
        txtstream.WriteLine("    txtstream.WriteLine(""    white-Space: nowrap='nowrap';"")")
        txtstream.WriteLine("    txtstream.WriteLine(""}"")")
        txtstream.WriteLine("    txtstream.WriteLine(""h1 {"")")
        txtstream.WriteLine("    txtstream.WriteLine(""color: antiquewhite;"")")
        txtstream.WriteLine("    txtstream.WriteLine(""text-shadow: 1px 1px 1px black;"")")
        txtstream.WriteLine("    txtstream.WriteLine(""padding: 3px;"")")
        txtstream.WriteLine("    txtstream.WriteLine(""text-align: center;"")")
        txtstream.WriteLine("    txtstream.WriteLine(""box-shadow: inset 2px 2px 5px rgba(0,0,0,0.5), inset -2px -2px 5px rgba(255,255,255,0.5);"")")
        txtstream.WriteLine("    txtstream.WriteLine(""}"")")
        txtstream.WriteLine("    txtstream.WriteLine(""</style>"")")

    '

        Case "Oscillating Row Colors"


        txtstream.WriteLine("    txtstream.WriteLine(""<style type='text/css'>"")")
        txtstream.WriteLine("    txtstream.WriteLine(""th"")")
        txtstream.WriteLine("    txtstream.WriteLine(""{"")")
        txtstream.WriteLine("    txtstream.WriteLine(""    COLOR: white;"")")
        txtstream.WriteLine("    txtstream.WriteLine(""    BACKGROUND-COLOR: navy;"")")
        txtstream.WriteLine("    txtstream.WriteLine(""    FONT-FAMILY:font-family: Cambria, serif;"")")
        txtstream.WriteLine("    txtstream.WriteLine(""    FONT-SIZE: 12px;"")")
        txtstream.WriteLine("    txtstream.WriteLine(""    text-align: left;"")")
```

```
        txtstream.WriteLine("     txtstream.WriteLine(""   white-Space:
nowrap='nowrap';"")")
        txtstream.WriteLine("     txtstream.WriteLine(""}"")")
        txtstream.WriteLine("     txtstream.WriteLine(""td"")")
        txtstream.WriteLine("     txtstream.WriteLine(""{"")")
        txtstream.WriteLine("     txtstream.WriteLine(""   COLOR: navy;"")")
        txtstream.WriteLine("     txtstream.WriteLine(""   FONT-FAMILY: font-
family: Cambria, serif;"")")
        txtstream.WriteLine("     txtstream.WriteLine(""   FONT-SIZE: 12px;"")")
        txtstream.WriteLine("     txtstream.WriteLine(""   text-align: left;"")")
        txtstream.WriteLine("     txtstream.WriteLine(""   white-Space:
nowrap='nowrap';"")")
        txtstream.WriteLine("     txtstream.WriteLine(""}"")")
        txtstream.WriteLine("     txtstream.WriteLine(""div"")")
        txtstream.WriteLine("     txtstream.WriteLine(""{"")")
        txtstream.WriteLine("     txtstream.WriteLine(""   COLOR: navy;"")")
        txtstream.WriteLine("     txtstream.WriteLine(""   FONT-FAMILY: font-
family: Cambria, serif;"")")
        txtstream.WriteLine("     txtstream.WriteLine(""   FONT-SIZE: 12px;"")")
        txtstream.WriteLine("     txtstream.WriteLine(""   text-align: left;"")")
        txtstream.WriteLine("     txtstream.WriteLine(""   white-Space:
nowrap='nowrap';"")")
        txtstream.WriteLine("     txtstream.WriteLine(""}"")")
        txtstream.WriteLine("     txtstream.WriteLine(""span"")")
        txtstream.WriteLine("     txtstream.WriteLine(""{"")")
        txtstream.WriteLine("     txtstream.WriteLine(""   COLOR: navy;"")")
        txtstream.WriteLine("     txtstream.WriteLine(""   FONT-FAMILY: font-
family: Cambria, serif;"")")
        txtstream.WriteLine("     txtstream.WriteLine(""   FONT-SIZE: 12px;"")")
        txtstream.WriteLine("     txtstream.WriteLine(""   text-align: left;"")")
        txtstream.WriteLine("     txtstream.WriteLine(""   white-Space:
nowrap='nowrap';"")")
        txtstream.WriteLine("     txtstream.WriteLine(""   width: 100%;"")")
        txtstream.WriteLine("     txtstream.WriteLine(""}"")")
        txtstream.WriteLine("     txtstream.WriteLine(""textarea"")")
        txtstream.WriteLine("     txtstream.WriteLine(""{"")")
        txtstream.WriteLine("     txtstream.WriteLine(""   COLOR: navy;"")")
        txtstream.WriteLine("     txtstream.WriteLine(""   FONT-FAMILY: font-
family: Cambria, serif;"")")
        txtstream.WriteLine("     txtstream.WriteLine(""   FONT-SIZE: 12px;"")")
        txtstream.WriteLine("     txtstream.WriteLine(""   text-align: left;"")")
        txtstream.WriteLine("     txtstream.WriteLine(""   white-Space:
nowrap','"")")
        txtstream.WriteLine("     txtstream.WriteLine(""   display:inline-
block;"")")
        txtstream.WriteLine("     txtstream.WriteLine(""   width: 100%;"")")
        txtstream.WriteLine("     txtstream.WriteLine(""}"")")
        txtstream.WriteLine("     txtstream.WriteLine(""select"")")
        txtstream.WriteLine("     txtstream.WriteLine(""{"")")
        txtstream.WriteLine("     txtstream.WriteLine(""   COLOR: navy;"")")
```

```
            txtstream.WriteLine("   txtstream.WriteLine("""    FONT-FAMILY: font-
family: Cambria, serif;""")")
            txtstream.WriteLine("   txtstream.WriteLine("""    FONT-SIZE: 10px;""")")
            txtstream.WriteLine("   txtstream.WriteLine("""    text-align: left;""")")
            txtstream.WriteLine("   txtstream.WriteLine("""    white-Space:
nowrap='nowrap';""")")
            txtstream.WriteLine("   txtstream.WriteLine("""    display:inline-
block;""")")
            txtstream.WriteLine("   txtstream.WriteLine("""    width: 100%;""")")
            txtstream.WriteLine("   txtstream.WriteLine("""}""")")
            txtstream.WriteLine("   txtstream.WriteLine("""input""")")
            txtstream.WriteLine("   txtstream.WriteLine("""{""")")
            txtstream.WriteLine("   txtstream.WriteLine("""    COLOR: navy;""")")
            txtstream.WriteLine("   txtstream.WriteLine("""    FONT-FAMILY: font-
family: Cambria, serif;""")")
            txtstream.WriteLine("   txtstream.WriteLine("""    FONT-SIZE: 12px;""")")
            txtstream.WriteLine("   txtstream.WriteLine("""    text-align: left;""")")
            txtstream.WriteLine("   txtstream.WriteLine("""    display:table-cell;""")")
            txtstream.WriteLine("   txtstream.WriteLine("""    white-Space:
nowrap='nowrap';""")")
            txtstream.WriteLine("   txtstream.WriteLine("""}""")")
            txtstream.WriteLine("   txtstream.WriteLine("""h1 {""")")
            txtstream.WriteLine("   txtstream.WriteLine("""color: antiquewhite;""")")
            txtstream.WriteLine("   txtstream.WriteLine("""text-shadow: 1px 1px 1px
black;""")")
            txtstream.WriteLine("   txtstream.WriteLine("""padding: 3px;""")")
            txtstream.WriteLine("   txtstream.WriteLine("""text-align: center;""")")
            txtstream.WriteLine("   txtstream.WriteLine("""box-shadow: inset 2px 2px
5px rgba(0,0,0,0.5), inset -2px -2px 5px rgba(255,255,255,0.5);""")")
            txtstream.WriteLine("   txtstream.WriteLine("""}""")")
            txtstream.WriteLine("   txtstream.WriteLine("""tr:nth-
child(even){background-color:#f2f2f2;}""")")
            txtstream.WriteLine("   txtstream.WriteLine("""tr:nth-
child(odd){background-color:#cccccc; color:#f2f2f2;}""")")
            txtstream.WriteLine("   txtstream.WriteLine("""</style>""")")

        Case "Ghost Decorated"

            txtstream.WriteLine("   txtstream.WriteLine("""<style
type='text/css'>""")")
            txtstream.WriteLine("   txtstream.WriteLine("""th""")")
            txtstream.WriteLine("   txtstream.WriteLine("""{""")")
            txtstream.WriteLine("   txtstream.WriteLine("""    COLOR: black;""")")
            txtstream.WriteLine("   txtstream.WriteLine("""    BACKGROUND-COLOR:
white;""")")
            txtstream.WriteLine("   txtstream.WriteLine("""    FONT-FAMILY:font-
family: Cambria, serif;""")")
            txtstream.WriteLine("   txtstream.WriteLine("""    FONT-SIZE: 12px;""")")
            txtstream.WriteLine("   txtstream.WriteLine("""    text-align: left;""")")
```

```
        txtstream.WriteLine("    txtstream.WriteLine("""    white-Space:
nowrap='nowrap';""")")
        txtstream.WriteLine("    txtstream.WriteLine("""}""")")
        txtstream.WriteLine("    txtstream.WriteLine("""td""")")
        txtstream.WriteLine("    txtstream.WriteLine("""{""")")
        txtstream.WriteLine("    txtstream.WriteLine("""    COLOR: black;""")")
        txtstream.WriteLine("    txtstream.WriteLine("""    BACKGROUND-COLOR:
white;""")")
        txtstream.WriteLine("    txtstream.WriteLine("""    FONT-FAMILY: font-
family: Cambria, serif;""")")
        txtstream.WriteLine("    txtstream.WriteLine("""    FONT-SIZE: 12px;""")")
        txtstream.WriteLine("    txtstream.WriteLine("""    text-align: left;""")")
        txtstream.WriteLine("    txtstream.WriteLine("""    white-Space:
nowrap='nowrap';""")")
        txtstream.WriteLine("    txtstream.WriteLine("""}""")")
        txtstream.WriteLine("    txtstream.WriteLine("""div""")")
        txtstream.WriteLine("    txtstream.WriteLine("""{""")")
        txtstream.WriteLine("    txtstream.WriteLine("""    COLOR: black;""")")
        txtstream.WriteLine("    txtstream.WriteLine("""    BACKGROUND-COLOR:
white;""")")
        txtstream.WriteLine("    txtstream.WriteLine("""    FONT-FAMILY: font-
family: Cambria, serif;""")")
        txtstream.WriteLine("    txtstream.WriteLine("""    FONT-SIZE: 10px;""")")
        txtstream.WriteLine("    txtstream.WriteLine("""    text-align: left;""")")
        txtstream.WriteLine("    txtstream.WriteLine("""    white-Space:
nowrap='nowrap';""")")
        txtstream.WriteLine("    txtstream.WriteLine("""}""")")
        txtstream.WriteLine("    txtstream.WriteLine("""span""")")
        txtstream.WriteLine("    txtstream.WriteLine("""{""")")
        txtstream.WriteLine("    txtstream.WriteLine("""    COLOR: black;""")")
        txtstream.WriteLine("    txtstream.WriteLine("""    BACKGROUND-COLOR:
white;""")")
        txtstream.WriteLine("    txtstream.WriteLine("""    FONT-FAMILY: font-
family: Cambria, serif;""")")
        txtstream.WriteLine("    txtstream.WriteLine("""    FONT-SIZE: 10px;""")")
        txtstream.WriteLine("    txtstream.WriteLine("""    text-align: left;""")")
        txtstream.WriteLine("    txtstream.WriteLine("""    white-Space:
nowrap='nowrap';""")")
        txtstream.WriteLine("    txtstream.WriteLine("""    display:inline-
block;""")")
        txtstream.WriteLine("    txtstream.WriteLine("""    width: 100%;""")")
        txtstream.WriteLine("    txtstream.WriteLine("""}""")")
        txtstream.WriteLine("    txtstream.WriteLine("""textarea""")")
        txtstream.WriteLine("    txtstream.WriteLine("""{""")")
        txtstream.WriteLine("    txtstream.WriteLine("""    COLOR: black;""")")
        txtstream.WriteLine("    txtstream.WriteLine("""    BACKGROUND-COLOR:
white;""")")
        txtstream.WriteLine("    txtstream.WriteLine("""    FONT-FAMILY: font-
family: Cambria, serif;""")")
        txtstream.WriteLine("    txtstream.WriteLine("""    FONT-SIZE: 10px;""")")
```

```
        txtstream.WriteLine("   txtstream.WriteLine("""   text-align: left;""")")
        txtstream.WriteLine("   txtstream.WriteLine("""   white-Space:
nowrap='nowrap';""")")
        txtstream.WriteLine("   txtstream.WriteLine("""   width: 100%;""")")
        txtstream.WriteLine("   txtstream.WriteLine("""}""")")
        txtstream.WriteLine("   txtstream.WriteLine("""select""")")
        txtstream.WriteLine("   txtstream.WriteLine("""{""")")
        txtstream.WriteLine("   txtstream.WriteLine("""   COLOR: black;""")")
        txtstream.WriteLine("   txtstream.WriteLine("""   BACKGROUND-COLOR:
white;""")")
        txtstream.WriteLine("   txtstream.WriteLine("""   FONT-FAMILY: font-
family: Cambria, serif;""")")
        txtstream.WriteLine("   txtstream.WriteLine("""   FONT-SIZE: 10px;""")")
        txtstream.WriteLine("   txtstream.WriteLine("""   text-align: left;""")")
        txtstream.WriteLine("   txtstream.WriteLine("""   white-Space:
nowrap='nowrap';""")")
        txtstream.WriteLine("   txtstream.WriteLine("""   width: 100%;""")")
        txtstream.WriteLine("   txtstream.WriteLine("""}""")")
        txtstream.WriteLine("   txtstream.WriteLine("""input""")")
        txtstream.WriteLine("   txtstream.WriteLine("""{""")")
        txtstream.WriteLine("   txtstream.WriteLine("""   COLOR: black;""")")
        txtstream.WriteLine("   txtstream.WriteLine("""   BACKGROUND-COLOR:
white;""")")
        txtstream.WriteLine("   txtstream.WriteLine("""   FONT-FAMILY: font-
family: Cambria, serif;""")")
        txtstream.WriteLine("   txtstream.WriteLine("""   FONT-SIZE: 12px;""")")
        txtstream.WriteLine("   txtstream.WriteLine("""   text-align: left;""")")
        txtstream.WriteLine("   txtstream.WriteLine("""   display:table-cell;""")")
        txtstream.WriteLine("   txtstream.WriteLine("""   white-Space:
nowrap='nowrap';""")")
        txtstream.WriteLine("   txtstream.WriteLine("""}""")")
        txtstream.WriteLine("   txtstream.WriteLine("""h1 {""")")
        txtstream.WriteLine("   txtstream.WriteLine("""color: antiquewhite;""")")
        txtstream.WriteLine("   txtstream.WriteLine("""text-shadow: 1px 1px 1px
black;""")")
        txtstream.WriteLine("   txtstream.WriteLine("""padding: 3px;""")")
        txtstream.WriteLine("   txtstream.WriteLine("""text-align: center;""")")
        txtstream.WriteLine("   txtstream.WriteLine("""box-shadow: inset 2px 2px
5px rgba(0,0,0,0.5), inset -2px -2px 5px rgba(255,255,255,0.5);""")")
        txtstream.WriteLine("   txtstream.WriteLine("""}""")")
        txtstream.WriteLine("   txtstream.WriteLine("""</style>""")")


    Case "3D"


        txtstream.WriteLine("   txtstream.WriteLine("""<style
type='text/css'>""")")
        txtstream.WriteLine("   txtstream.WriteLine("""body""")")
        txtstream.WriteLine("   txtstream.WriteLine("""{""")")
```

```
        txtstream.WriteLine("        txtstream.WriteLine(""    PADDING-RIGHT:
0px;""")")
        txtstream.WriteLine("        txtstream.WriteLine(""    PADDING-LEFT:
0px;""")")
        txtstream.WriteLine("        txtstream.WriteLine(""    PADDING-BOTTOM:
0px;""")")
        txtstream.WriteLine("        txtstream.WriteLine(""    MARGIN: 0px;""")")
        txtstream.WriteLine("        txtstream.WriteLine(""    COLOR: #333;""")")
        txtstream.WriteLine("        txtstream.WriteLine(""    PADDING-TOP:
0px;""")")
        txtstream.WriteLine("        txtstream.WriteLine(""    FONT-FAMILY: verdana,
arial, helvetica, sans-serif;""")")
        txtstream.WriteLine("        txtstream.WriteLine(""}""")")
        txtstream.WriteLine("        txtstream.WriteLine(""table""")")
        txtstream.WriteLine("        txtstream.WriteLine(""{""")")
        txtstream.WriteLine("        txtstream.WriteLine(""    BORDER-RIGHT:
#999999 3px solid;""")")
        txtstream.WriteLine("        txtstream.WriteLine(""    PADDING-RIGHT:
6px;""")")
        txtstream.WriteLine("        txtstream.WriteLine(""    PADDING-LEFT:
6px;""")")
        txtstream.WriteLine("        txtstream.WriteLine(""    FONT-WEIGHT:
Bold;""")")
        txtstream.WriteLine("        txtstream.WriteLine(""    FONT-SIZE: 14px;""")")
        txtstream.WriteLine("        txtstream.WriteLine(""    PADDING-BOTTOM:
6px;""")")
        txtstream.WriteLine("        txtstream.WriteLine(""    COLOR: Peru;""")")
        txtstream.WriteLine("        txtstream.WriteLine(""    LINE-HEIGHT:
14px;""")")
        txtstream.WriteLine("        txtstream.WriteLine(""    PADDING-TOP:
6px;""")")
        txtstream.WriteLine("        txtstream.WriteLine(""    BORDER-BOTTOM:
#999 1px solid;""")")
        txtstream.WriteLine("        txtstream.WriteLine(""    BACKGROUND-COLOR:
#eeeeee;""")")
        txtstream.WriteLine("        txtstream.WriteLine(""    FONT-FAMILY: verdana,
arial, helvetica, sans-serif;""")")
        txtstream.WriteLine("        txtstream.WriteLine(""    FONT-SIZE: 12px;""")")
        txtstream.WriteLine("        txtstream.WriteLine(""}""")")
        txtstream.WriteLine("        txtstream.WriteLine(""th""")")
        txtstream.WriteLine("        txtstream.WriteLine(""{""")")
        txtstream.WriteLine("        txtstream.WriteLine(""    BORDER-RIGHT:
#999999 3px solid;""")")
        txtstream.WriteLine("        txtstream.WriteLine(""    PADDING-RIGHT:
6px;""")")
        txtstream.WriteLine("        txtstream.WriteLine(""    PADDING-LEFT:
6px;""")")
        txtstream.WriteLine("        txtstream.WriteLine(""    FONT-WEIGHT:
Bold;""")")
        txtstream.WriteLine("        txtstream.WriteLine(""    FONT-SIZE: 14px;""")")
```

```
txtstream.WriteLine("   txtstream.WriteLine("""   PADDING-BOTTOM: 6px;""")")
txtstream.WriteLine("   txtstream.WriteLine("""   COLOR: darkred;""")")
txtstream.WriteLine("   txtstream.WriteLine("""   LINE-HEIGHT: 14px;""")")
txtstream.WriteLine("   txtstream.WriteLine("""   PADDING-TOP: 6px;""")")
txtstream.WriteLine("   txtstream.WriteLine("""   BORDER-BOTTOM: #999 1px solid;""")")
txtstream.WriteLine("   txtstream.WriteLine("""   BACKGROUND-COLOR: #eeeeee;""")")
txtstream.WriteLine("   txtstream.WriteLine("""   FONT-FAMILY:font-family: Cambria, serif;""")")
txtstream.WriteLine("   txtstream.WriteLine("""   FONT-SIZE: 12px;""")")
txtstream.WriteLine("   txtstream.WriteLine("""   text-align: left;""")")
txtstream.WriteLine("   txtstream.WriteLine("""   white-Space: nowrap='nowrap';""")")
txtstream.WriteLine("   txtstream.WriteLine("""}""")")
txtstream.WriteLine("   txtstream.WriteLine(""".th""")")
txtstream.WriteLine("   txtstream.WriteLine("""{""")")
txtstream.WriteLine("   txtstream.WriteLine("""   BORDER-RIGHT: #999999 2px solid;""")")
txtstream.WriteLine("   txtstream.WriteLine("""   PADDING-RIGHT: 6px;""")")
txtstream.WriteLine("   txtstream.WriteLine("""   PADDING-LEFT: 6px;""")")
txtstream.WriteLine("   txtstream.WriteLine("""   FONT-WEIGHT: Bold;""")")
txtstream.WriteLine("   txtstream.WriteLine("""   PADDING-BOTTOM: 6px;""")")
txtstream.WriteLine("   txtstream.WriteLine("""   COLOR: black;""")")
txtstream.WriteLine("   txtstream.WriteLine("""   PADDING-TOP: 6px;""")")
txtstream.WriteLine("   txtstream.WriteLine("""   BORDER-BOTTOM: #999 2px solid;""")")
txtstream.WriteLine("   txtstream.WriteLine("""   BACKGROUND-COLOR: #eeeeee;""")")
txtstream.WriteLine("   txtstream.WriteLine("""   FONT-FAMILY: font-family: Cambria, serif;""")")
txtstream.WriteLine("   txtstream.WriteLine("""   FONT-SIZE: 10px;""")")
txtstream.WriteLine("   txtstream.WriteLine("""   text-align: right;""")")
txtstream.WriteLine("   txtstream.WriteLine("""   white-Space: nowrap='nowrap';""")")
txtstream.WriteLine("   txtstream.WriteLine("""}""")")
txtstream.WriteLine("   txtstream.WriteLine("""td""")")
txtstream.WriteLine("   txtstream.WriteLine("""{""")")
txtstream.WriteLine("   txtstream.WriteLine("""   BORDER-RIGHT: #999999 3px solid;""")")
txtstream.WriteLine("   txtstream.WriteLine("""   PADDING-RIGHT: 6px;""")")
```

```
        txtstream.WriteLine("    txtstream.WriteLine(""    PADDING-LEFT:
6px;"")")
        txtstream.WriteLine("    txtstream.WriteLine(""    FONT-WEIGHT:
Normal;"")")
        txtstream.WriteLine("    txtstream.WriteLine(""    PADDING-BOTTOM:
6px;"")")
        txtstream.WriteLine("    txtstream.WriteLine(""    COLOR: navy;"")")
        txtstream.WriteLine("    txtstream.WriteLine(""    LINE-HEIGHT:
14px;"")")
        txtstream.WriteLine("    txtstream.WriteLine(""    PADDING-TOP:
6px;"")")
        txtstream.WriteLine("    txtstream.WriteLine(""    BORDER-BOTTOM:
#999 1px solid;"")")
        txtstream.WriteLine("    txtstream.WriteLine(""    BACKGROUND-COLOR:
#eeeeee;"")")
        txtstream.WriteLine("    txtstream.WriteLine(""    FONT-FAMILY: font-
family: Cambria, serif;"")")
        txtstream.WriteLine("    txtstream.WriteLine(""    FONT-SIZE: 12px;"")")
        txtstream.WriteLine("    txtstream.WriteLine(""    text-align: left;"")")
        txtstream.WriteLine("    txtstream.WriteLine(""    white-Space:
nowrap='nowrap';"")")
        txtstream.WriteLine("    txtstream.WriteLine(""}"")")
        txtstream.WriteLine("    txtstream.WriteLine(""div"")")
        txtstream.WriteLine("    txtstream.WriteLine(""{"")")
        txtstream.WriteLine("    txtstream.WriteLine(""    BORDER-RIGHT:
#999999 3px solid;"")")
        txtstream.WriteLine("    txtstream.WriteLine(""    PADDING-RIGHT:
6px;"")")
        txtstream.WriteLine("    txtstream.WriteLine(""    PADDING-LEFT:
6px;"")")
        txtstream.WriteLine("    txtstream.WriteLine(""    FONT-WEIGHT:
Normal;"")")
        txtstream.WriteLine("    txtstream.WriteLine(""    PADDING-BOTTOM:
6px;"")")
        txtstream.WriteLine("    txtstream.WriteLine(""    COLOR: white;"")")
        txtstream.WriteLine("    txtstream.WriteLine(""    PADDING-TOP:
6px;"")")
        txtstream.WriteLine("    txtstream.WriteLine(""    BORDER-BOTTOM:
#999 1px solid;"")")
        txtstream.WriteLine("    txtstream.WriteLine(""    BACKGROUND-COLOR:
navy;"")")
        txtstream.WriteLine("    txtstream.WriteLine(""    FONT-FAMILY: font-
family: Cambria, serif;"")")
        txtstream.WriteLine("    txtstream.WriteLine(""    FONT-SIZE: 10px;"")")
        txtstream.WriteLine("    txtstream.WriteLine(""    text-align: left;"")")
        txtstream.WriteLine("    txtstream.WriteLine(""    white-Space:
nowrap='nowrap';"")")
        txtstream.WriteLine("    txtstream.WriteLine(""}"")")
        txtstream.WriteLine("    txtstream.WriteLine(""span"")")
        txtstream.WriteLine("    txtstream.WriteLine(""{"")")
```

```
        txtstream.WriteLine("        txtstream.WriteLine(""   BORDER-RIGHT:
#999999 3px solid;""")")
        txtstream.WriteLine("        txtstream.WriteLine("""   PADDING-RIGHT:
3px;""")")
        txtstream.WriteLine("        txtstream.WriteLine("""   PADDING-LEFT:
3px;""")")
        txtstream.WriteLine("        txtstream.WriteLine("""   FONT-WEIGHT:
Normal;""")")
        txtstream.WriteLine("        txtstream.WriteLine("""   PADDING-BOTTOM:
3px;""")")
        txtstream.WriteLine("        txtstream.WriteLine("""   COLOR: white;""")")
        txtstream.WriteLine("        txtstream.WriteLine("""   PADDING-TOP:
3px;""")")
        txtstream.WriteLine("        txtstream.WriteLine("""   BORDER-BOTTOM:
#999 1px solid;""")")
        txtstream.WriteLine("        txtstream.WriteLine("""   BACKGROUND-COLOR:
navy;""")")
        txtstream.WriteLine("        txtstream.WriteLine("""   FONT-FAMILY: font-
family: Cambria, serif;""")")
        txtstream.WriteLine("        txtstream.WriteLine("""   FONT-SIZE: 10px;""")")
        txtstream.WriteLine("        txtstream.WriteLine("""   text-align: left;""")")
        txtstream.WriteLine("        txtstream.WriteLine("""   white-Space:
nowrap='nowrap';""")")
        txtstream.WriteLine("        txtstream.WriteLine("""   display:inline-
block;""")")
        txtstream.WriteLine("        txtstream.WriteLine("""   width: 100%;""")")
        txtstream.WriteLine("        txtstream.WriteLine("""}""")")
        txtstream.WriteLine("        txtstream.WriteLine(""""textarea""")")
        txtstream.WriteLine("        txtstream.WriteLine("""{""")")
        txtstream.WriteLine("        txtstream.WriteLine("""   BORDER-RIGHT:
#999999 3px solid;""")")
        txtstream.WriteLine("        txtstream.WriteLine("""   PADDING-RIGHT:
3px;""")")
        txtstream.WriteLine("        txtstream.WriteLine("""   PADDING-LEFT:
3px;""")")
        txtstream.WriteLine("        txtstream.WriteLine("""   FONT-WEIGHT:
Normal;""")")
        txtstream.WriteLine("        txtstream.WriteLine("""   PADDING-BOTTOM:
3px;""")")
        txtstream.WriteLine("        txtstream.WriteLine("""   COLOR: white;""")")
        txtstream.WriteLine("        txtstream.WriteLine("""   PADDING-TOP:
3px;""")")
        txtstream.WriteLine("        txtstream.WriteLine("""   BORDER-BOTTOM:
#999 1px solid;""")")
        txtstream.WriteLine("        txtstream.WriteLine("""   BACKGROUND-COLOR:
navy;""")")
        txtstream.WriteLine("        txtstream.WriteLine("""   FONT-FAMILY: font-
family: Cambria, serif;""")")
        txtstream.WriteLine("        txtstream.WriteLine("""   FONT-SIZE: 10px;""")")
        txtstream.WriteLine("        txtstream.WriteLine("""   text-align: left;""")")
```

```
            txtstream.WriteLine("     txtstream.WriteLine(""    white-Space:
nowrap='nowrap';"")")
            txtstream.WriteLine("     txtstream.WriteLine(""    width: 100%;"")")
            txtstream.WriteLine("     txtstream.WriteLine(""}"")")
            txtstream.WriteLine("     txtstream.WriteLine(""select"")")
            txtstream.WriteLine("     txtstream.WriteLine(""{"")")
            txtstream.WriteLine("     txtstream.WriteLine(""    BORDER-RIGHT:
#999999 3px solid;"")")
            txtstream.WriteLine("     txtstream.WriteLine(""    PADDING-RIGHT:
6px;"")")
            txtstream.WriteLine("     txtstream.WriteLine(""    PADDING-LEFT:
6px;"")")
            txtstream.WriteLine("     txtstream.WriteLine(""    FONT-WEIGHT:
Normal;"")")
            txtstream.WriteLine("     txtstream.WriteLine(""    PADDING-BOTTOM:
6px;"")")
            txtstream.WriteLine("     txtstream.WriteLine(""    COLOR: white;"")")
            txtstream.WriteLine("     txtstream.WriteLine(""    PADDING-TOP:
6px;"")")
            txtstream.WriteLine("     txtstream.WriteLine(""    BORDER-BOTTOM:
#999 1px solid;"")")
            txtstream.WriteLine("     txtstream.WriteLine(""    BACKGROUND-COLOR:
navy;"")")
            txtstream.WriteLine("     txtstream.WriteLine(""    FONT-FAMILY: font-
family: Cambria, serif;"")")
            txtstream.WriteLine("     txtstream.WriteLine(""    FONT-SIZE: 10px;"")")
            txtstream.WriteLine("     txtstream.WriteLine(""    text-align: left;"")")
            txtstream.WriteLine("     txtstream.WriteLine(""    white-Space:
nowrap='nowrap';"")")
            txtstream.WriteLine("     txtstream.WriteLine(""    width: 100%;"")")
            txtstream.WriteLine("     txtstream.WriteLine(""}"")")
            txtstream.WriteLine("     txtstream.WriteLine(""input"")")
            txtstream.WriteLine("     txtstream.WriteLine(""{"")")
            txtstream.WriteLine("     txtstream.WriteLine(""    BORDER-RIGHT:
#999999 3px solid;"")")
            txtstream.WriteLine("     txtstream.WriteLine(""    PADDING-RIGHT:
3px;"")")
            txtstream.WriteLine("     txtstream.WriteLine(""    PADDING-LEFT:
3px;"")")
            txtstream.WriteLine("     txtstream.WriteLine(""    FONT-WEIGHT:
Bold;"")")
            txtstream.WriteLine("     txtstream.WriteLine(""    PADDING-BOTTOM:
3px;"")")
            txtstream.WriteLine("     txtstream.WriteLine(""    COLOR: white;"")")
            txtstream.WriteLine("     txtstream.WriteLine(""    PADDING-TOP:
3px;"")")
            txtstream.WriteLine("     txtstream.WriteLine(""    BORDER-BOTTOM:
#999 1px solid;"")")
            txtstream.WriteLine("     txtstream.WriteLine(""    BACKGROUND-COLOR:
navy;"")")
```

```
        txtstream.WriteLine("    txtstream.WriteLine(""    FONT-FAMILY: font-
family: Cambria, serif;"")")
        txtstream.WriteLine("    txtstream.WriteLine(""    FONT-SIZE: 12px;"")")
        txtstream.WriteLine("    txtstream.WriteLine(""    text-align: left;"")")
        txtstream.WriteLine("    txtstream.WriteLine(""    display:table-cell;"")")
        txtstream.WriteLine("    txtstream.WriteLine(""    white-Space:
nowrap='nowrap';"")")
        txtstream.WriteLine("    txtstream.WriteLine(""    width: 100%;"")")
        txtstream.WriteLine("    txtstream.WriteLine(""}"")")
        txtstream.WriteLine("    txtstream.WriteLine(""h1 {"")")
        txtstream.WriteLine("    txtstream.WriteLine(""color: antiquewhite;"")")
        txtstream.WriteLine("    txtstream.WriteLine(""text-shadow: 1px 1px 1px
black;"")")
        txtstream.WriteLine("    txtstream.WriteLine(""padding: 3px;"")")
        txtstream.WriteLine("    txtstream.WriteLine(""text-align: center;"")")
        txtstream.WriteLine("    txtstream.WriteLine(""box-shadow: inset 2px 2px
5px rgba(0,0,0,0.5), inset -2px -2px 5px rgba(255,255,255,0.5);"")")
        txtstream.WriteLine("    txtstream.WriteLine(""}"")")
        txtstream.WriteLine("    txtstream.WriteLine(""</style>"")")

        Case "Shadow Box"

        txtstream.WriteLine("    txtstream.WriteLine(""<style
type='text/css'>"")")
        txtstream.WriteLine("    txtstream.WriteLine(""body"")")
        txtstream.WriteLine("    txtstream.WriteLine(""{"")")
        txtstream.WriteLine("    txtstream.WriteLine(""    PADDING-RIGHT:
0px;"")")
        txtstream.WriteLine("    txtstream.WriteLine(""    PADDING-LEFT:
0px;"")")
        txtstream.WriteLine("    txtstream.WriteLine(""    PADDING-BOTTOM:
0px;"")")
        txtstream.WriteLine("    txtstream.WriteLine(""    MARGIN: 0px;"")")
        txtstream.WriteLine("    txtstream.WriteLine(""    COLOR: #333;"")")
        txtstream.WriteLine("    txtstream.WriteLine(""    PADDING-TOP:
0px;"")")
        txtstream.WriteLine("    txtstream.WriteLine(""    FONT-FAMILY: verdana,
arial, helvetica, sans-serif;"")")
        txtstream.WriteLine("    txtstream.WriteLine(""}"")")
        txtstream.WriteLine("    txtstream.WriteLine(""table"")")
        txtstream.WriteLine("    txtstream.WriteLine(""{"")")
        txtstream.WriteLine("    txtstream.WriteLine(""    BORDER-RIGHT:
#999999 1px solid;"")")
        txtstream.WriteLine("    txtstream.WriteLine(""    PADDING-RIGHT:
1px;"")")
        txtstream.WriteLine("    txtstream.WriteLine(""    PADDING-LEFT:
1px;"")")
        txtstream.WriteLine("    txtstream.WriteLine(""    PADDING-BOTTOM:
1px;"")")
```

```
txtstream.WriteLine("    txtstream.WriteLine(""   LINE-HEIGHT: 8px;"")")
txtstream.WriteLine("    txtstream.WriteLine(""   PADDING-TOP: 1px;"")")
txtstream.WriteLine("    txtstream.WriteLine(""   BORDER-BOTTOM: #999 1px solid;"")")
txtstream.WriteLine("    txtstream.WriteLine(""   BACKGROUND-COLOR: #eeeeee;"")")
txtstream.WriteLine("    txtstream.WriteLine(""   filter:progid:DXImageTransform.Microsoft.Shadow(color='silver', Direction=135, Strength=16)"")")
txtstream.WriteLine("    txtstream.WriteLine(""}"")")
txtstream.WriteLine("    txtstream.WriteLine(""th"")")
txtstream.WriteLine("    txtstream.WriteLine(""{"")")
txtstream.WriteLine("    txtstream.WriteLine(""   BORDER-RIGHT: #999999 3px solid;"")")
txtstream.WriteLine("    txtstream.WriteLine(""   PADDING-RIGHT: 6px;"")")
txtstream.WriteLine("    txtstream.WriteLine(""   PADDING-LEFT: 6px;"")")
txtstream.WriteLine("    txtstream.WriteLine(""   FONT-WEIGHT: Bold;"")")
txtstream.WriteLine("    txtstream.WriteLine(""   FONT-SIZE: 14px;"")")
txtstream.WriteLine("    txtstream.WriteLine(""   PADDING-BOTTOM: 6px;"")")
txtstream.WriteLine("    txtstream.WriteLine(""   COLOR: darkred;"")")
txtstream.WriteLine("    txtstream.WriteLine(""   LINE-HEIGHT: 14px;"")")
txtstream.WriteLine("    txtstream.WriteLine(""   PADDING-TOP: 6px;"")")
txtstream.WriteLine("    txtstream.WriteLine(""   BORDER-BOTTOM: #999 1px solid;"")")
txtstream.WriteLine("    txtstream.WriteLine(""   BACKGROUND-COLOR: #eeeeee;"")")
txtstream.WriteLine("    txtstream.WriteLine(""   FONT-FAMILY: font-family: Cambria, serif;"")")
txtstream.WriteLine("    txtstream.WriteLine(""   FONT-SIZE: 12px;"")")
txtstream.WriteLine("    txtstream.WriteLine(""   text-align: left;"")")
txtstream.WriteLine("    txtstream.WriteLine(""   white-Space: nowrap='nowrap';"")")
txtstream.WriteLine("    txtstream.WriteLine(""}"")")
txtstream.WriteLine("    txtstream.WriteLine("".th"")")
txtstream.WriteLine("    txtstream.WriteLine(""{"")")
txtstream.WriteLine("    txtstream.WriteLine(""   BORDER-RIGHT: #999999 2px solid;"")")
txtstream.WriteLine("    txtstream.WriteLine(""   PADDING-RIGHT: 6px;"")")
txtstream.WriteLine("    txtstream.WriteLine(""   PADDING-LEFT: 6px;"")")
```

```
        txtstream.WriteLine("       txtstream.WriteLine(""    FONT-WEIGHT:
Bold;""")")
        txtstream.WriteLine("       txtstream.WriteLine(""    PADDING-BOTTOM:
6px;""")")
        txtstream.WriteLine("       txtstream.WriteLine(""    COLOR: black;""")")
        txtstream.WriteLine("       txtstream.WriteLine(""    PADDING-TOP:
6px;""")")
        txtstream.WriteLine("       txtstream.WriteLine(""    BORDER-BOTTOM:
#999 2px solid;""")")
        txtstream.WriteLine("       txtstream.WriteLine(""    BACKGROUND-COLOR:
#eeeeee;""")")
        txtstream.WriteLine("       txtstream.WriteLine(""    FONT-FAMILY: font-
family: Cambria, serif;""")")
        txtstream.WriteLine("       txtstream.WriteLine(""    FONT-SIZE: 10px;""")")
        txtstream.WriteLine("       txtstream.WriteLine(""    text-align: right;""")")
        txtstream.WriteLine("       txtstream.WriteLine(""    white-Space:
nowrap='nowrap';""")")
        txtstream.WriteLine("       txtstream.WriteLine(""}""")")
        txtstream.WriteLine("       txtstream.WriteLine(""td""")")
        txtstream.WriteLine("       txtstream.WriteLine(""{""")")
        txtstream.WriteLine("       txtstream.WriteLine(""    BORDER-RIGHT:
#999999 3px solid;""")")
        txtstream.WriteLine("       txtstream.WriteLine(""    PADDING-RIGHT:
6px;""")")
        txtstream.WriteLine("       txtstream.WriteLine(""    PADDING-LEFT:
6px;""")")
        txtstream.WriteLine("       txtstream.WriteLine(""    FONT-WEIGHT:
Normal;""")")
        txtstream.WriteLine("       txtstream.WriteLine(""    PADDING-BOTTOM:
6px;""")")
        txtstream.WriteLine("       txtstream.WriteLine(""    COLOR: navy;""")")
        txtstream.WriteLine("       txtstream.WriteLine(""    LINE-HEIGHT:
14px;""")")
        txtstream.WriteLine("       txtstream.WriteLine(""    PADDING-TOP:
6px;""")")
        txtstream.WriteLine("       txtstream.WriteLine(""    BORDER-BOTTOM:
#999 1px solid;""")")
        txtstream.WriteLine("       txtstream.WriteLine(""    BACKGROUND-COLOR:
#eeeeee;""")")
        txtstream.WriteLine("       txtstream.WriteLine(""    FONT-FAMILY: font-
family: Cambria, serif;""")")
        txtstream.WriteLine("       txtstream.WriteLine(""    FONT-SIZE: 12px;""")")
        txtstream.WriteLine("       txtstream.WriteLine(""    text-align: left;""")")
        txtstream.WriteLine("       txtstream.WriteLine(""    white-Space:
nowrap='nowrap';""")")
        txtstream.WriteLine("       txtstream.WriteLine(""}""")")
        txtstream.WriteLine("       txtstream.WriteLine(""div""")")
        txtstream.WriteLine("       txtstream.WriteLine(""{""")")
        txtstream.WriteLine("       txtstream.WriteLine(""    BORDER-RIGHT:
#999999 3px solid;""")")
```

```
        txtstream.WriteLine("        txtstream.WriteLine(""        PADDING-RIGHT:
6px;""")")
        txtstream.WriteLine("        txtstream.WriteLine(""        PADDING-LEFT:
6px;""")")
        txtstream.WriteLine("        txtstream.WriteLine(""        FONT-WEIGHT:
Normal;""")")
        txtstream.WriteLine("        txtstream.WriteLine(""        PADDING-BOTTOM:
6px;""")")
        txtstream.WriteLine("        txtstream.WriteLine(""        COLOR: white;""")")
        txtstream.WriteLine("        txtstream.WriteLine(""        PADDING-TOP:
6px;""")")
        txtstream.WriteLine("        txtstream.WriteLine(""        BORDER-BOTTOM:
#999 1px solid;""")")
        txtstream.WriteLine("        txtstream.WriteLine(""        BACKGROUND-COLOR:
navy;""")")
        txtstream.WriteLine("        txtstream.WriteLine(""        FONT-FAMILY: font-
family: Cambria, serif;""")")
        txtstream.WriteLine("        txtstream.WriteLine(""        FONT-SIZE: 10px;""")")
        txtstream.WriteLine("        txtstream.WriteLine(""        text-align: left;""")")
        txtstream.WriteLine("        txtstream.WriteLine(""        white-Space:
nowrap='nowrap';""")")
        txtstream.WriteLine("        txtstream.WriteLine(""}""")")
        txtstream.WriteLine("        txtstream.WriteLine(""span""")")
        txtstream.WriteLine("        txtstream.WriteLine(""{""")")
        txtstream.WriteLine("        txtstream.WriteLine(""        BORDER-RIGHT:
#999999 3px solid;""")")
        txtstream.WriteLine("        txtstream.WriteLine(""        PADDING-RIGHT:
3px;""")")
        txtstream.WriteLine("        txtstream.WriteLine(""        PADDING-LEFT:
3px;""")")
        txtstream.WriteLine("        txtstream.WriteLine(""        FONT-WEIGHT:
Normal;""")")
        txtstream.WriteLine("        txtstream.WriteLine(""        PADDING-BOTTOM:
3px;""")")
        txtstream.WriteLine("        txtstream.WriteLine(""        COLOR: white;""")")
        txtstream.WriteLine("        txtstream.WriteLine(""        PADDING-TOP:
3px;""")")
        txtstream.WriteLine("        txtstream.WriteLine(""        BORDER-BOTTOM:
#999 1px solid;""")")
        txtstream.WriteLine("        txtstream.WriteLine(""        BACKGROUND-COLOR:
navy;""")")
        txtstream.WriteLine("        txtstream.WriteLine(""        FONT-FAMILY: font-
family: Cambria, serif;""")")
        txtstream.WriteLine("        txtstream.WriteLine(""        FONT-SIZE: 10px;""")")
        txtstream.WriteLine("        txtstream.WriteLine(""        text-align: left;""")")
        txtstream.WriteLine("        txtstream.WriteLine(""        white-Space:
nowrap='nowrap';""")")
        txtstream.WriteLine("        txtstream.WriteLine(""        display: inline-
block;""")")
        txtstream.WriteLine("        txtstream.WriteLine(""        width: 100%;""")")
```

```
txtstream.WriteLine("    txtstream.WriteLine("""}""")")
txtstream.WriteLine("    txtstream.WriteLine("""textarea""")")
txtstream.WriteLine("    txtstream.WriteLine("""{""")")
txtstream.WriteLine("    txtstream.WriteLine("""    BORDER-RIGHT: #999999 3px solid;""")")
txtstream.WriteLine("    txtstream.WriteLine("""    PADDING-RIGHT: 3px;""")")
txtstream.WriteLine("    txtstream.WriteLine("""    PADDING-LEFT: 3px;""")")
txtstream.WriteLine("    txtstream.WriteLine("""    FONT-WEIGHT: Normal;""")")
txtstream.WriteLine("    txtstream.WriteLine("""    PADDING-BOTTOM: 3px;""")")
txtstream.WriteLine("    txtstream.WriteLine("""    COLOR: white;""")")
txtstream.WriteLine("    txtstream.WriteLine("""    PADDING-TOP: 3px;""")")
txtstream.WriteLine("    txtstream.WriteLine("""    BORDER-BOTTOM: #999 1px solid;""")")
txtstream.WriteLine("    txtstream.WriteLine("""    BACKGROUND-COLOR: navy;""")")
txtstream.WriteLine("    txtstream.WriteLine("""    FONT-FAMILY: font-family: Cambria, serif;""")")
txtstream.WriteLine("    txtstream.WriteLine("""    FONT-SIZE: 10px;""")")
txtstream.WriteLine("    txtstream.WriteLine("""    text-align: left;""")")
txtstream.WriteLine("    txtstream.WriteLine("""    white-Space: nowrap='nowrap';""")")
txtstream.WriteLine("    txtstream.WriteLine("""    width: 100%;""")")
txtstream.WriteLine("    txtstream.WriteLine("""}""")")
txtstream.WriteLine("    txtstream.WriteLine("""select""")")
txtstream.WriteLine("    txtstream.WriteLine("""{""")")
txtstream.WriteLine("    txtstream.WriteLine("""    BORDER-RIGHT: #999999 3px solid;""")")
txtstream.WriteLine("    txtstream.WriteLine("""    PADDING-RIGHT: 6px;""")")
txtstream.WriteLine("    txtstream.WriteLine("""    PADDING-LEFT: 6px;""")")
txtstream.WriteLine("    txtstream.WriteLine("""    FONT-WEIGHT: Normal;""")")
txtstream.WriteLine("    txtstream.WriteLine("""    PADDING-BOTTOM: 6px;""")")
txtstream.WriteLine("    txtstream.WriteLine("""    COLOR: white;""")")
txtstream.WriteLine("    txtstream.WriteLine("""    PADDING-TOP: 6px;""")")
txtstream.WriteLine("    txtstream.WriteLine("""    BORDER-BOTTOM: #999 1px solid;""")")
txtstream.WriteLine("    txtstream.WriteLine("""    BACKGROUND-COLOR: navy;""")")
txtstream.WriteLine("    txtstream.WriteLine("""    FONT-FAMILY: font-family: Cambria, serif;""")")
txtstream.WriteLine("    txtstream.WriteLine("""    FONT-SIZE: 10px;""")")
```

```vbnet
        txtstream.WriteLine("    txtstream.WriteLine("""   text-align: left;""")")
        txtstream.WriteLine("    txtstream.WriteLine("""   white-Space:
nowrap='nowrap';""")")
        txtstream.WriteLine("    txtstream.WriteLine("""   width: 100%;""")")
        txtstream.WriteLine("    txtstream.WriteLine("""}""")")
        txtstream.WriteLine("    txtstream.WriteLine("""input""")")
        txtstream.WriteLine("    txtstream.WriteLine("""{""")")
        txtstream.WriteLine("    txtstream.WriteLine("""   BORDER-RIGHT:
#999999 3px solid;""")")
        txtstream.WriteLine("    txtstream.WriteLine("""   PADDING-RIGHT:
3px;""")")
        txtstream.WriteLine("    txtstream.WriteLine("""   PADDING-LEFT:
3px;""")")
        txtstream.WriteLine("    txtstream.WriteLine("""   FONT-WEIGHT:
Bold;""")")
        txtstream.WriteLine("    txtstream.WriteLine("""   PADDING-BOTTOM:
3px;""")")
        txtstream.WriteLine("    txtstream.WriteLine("""   COLOR: white;""")")
        txtstream.WriteLine("    txtstream.WriteLine("""   PADDING-TOP:
3px;""")")
        txtstream.WriteLine("    txtstream.WriteLine("""   BORDER-BOTTOM:
#999 1px solid;""")")
        txtstream.WriteLine("    txtstream.WriteLine("""   BACKGROUND-COLOR:
navy;""")")
        txtstream.WriteLine("    txtstream.WriteLine("""   FONT-FAMILY: font-
family: Cambria, serif;""")")
        txtstream.WriteLine("    txtstream.WriteLine("""   FONT-SIZE: 12px;""")")
        txtstream.WriteLine("    txtstream.WriteLine("""   text-align: left;""")")
        txtstream.WriteLine("    txtstream.WriteLine("""   display: table-cell;""")")
        txtstream.WriteLine("    txtstream.WriteLine("""   white-Space:
nowrap='nowrap';""")")
        txtstream.WriteLine("    txtstream.WriteLine("""   width: 100%;""")")
        txtstream.WriteLine("    txtstream.WriteLine("""}""")")
        txtstream.WriteLine("    txtstream.WriteLine("""h1 {""")")
        txtstream.WriteLine("    txtstream.WriteLine("""color: antiquewhite;""")")
        txtstream.WriteLine("    txtstream.WriteLine("""text-shadow: 1px 1px 1px
black;""")")
        txtstream.WriteLine("    txtstream.WriteLine("""padding: 3px;""")")
        txtstream.WriteLine("    txtstream.WriteLine("""text-align: center;""")")
        txtstream.WriteLine("    txtstream.WriteLine("""box-shadow: inset 2px 2px
5px rgba(0,0,0,0.5), inset -2px -2px 5px rgba(255,255,255,0.5);""")")
        txtstream.WriteLine("    txtstream.WriteLine("""}""")")
        txtstream.WriteLine("    txtstream.WriteLine("""</style>""")")


    End Select

    End Sub
```

Wrapping things up
Chapter Subtitle

At the end of this Module is the code need to finish and close the txtstream code.

Private Sub End_The_HTA_Code()

```
txtstream.WriteLine("    txtstream.WriteLine(""""</table>""")")
txtstream.WriteLine("    txtstream.WriteLine(""""</body>""")")
txtstream.WriteLine("    txtstream.WriteLine(""""</html>""")")
txtstream.Close()
```

End Sub

Private Sub End_The_HTML_Code()

```
txtstream.WriteLine("    txtstream.WriteLine(""""</table>""")")
txtstream.WriteLine("    txtstream.WriteLine(""""</body>""")")
txtstream.WriteLine("    txtstream.WriteLine(""""</html>""")")
txtstream.Close()
```

End Sub

Private Sub End_The_ASP_Code()

```vbnet
        txtstream.WriteLine("    txtstream.WriteLine(""%>"")")
        txtstream.WriteLine("    txtstream.WriteLine(""</table>"")")
        txtstream.WriteLine("    txtstream.WriteLine(""</body>"")")
        txtstream.WriteLine("    txtstream.WriteLine(""</html>"")")
        txtstream.Close()

    End Sub

    Private Sub End_The_ASPX_Code()

        txtstream.WriteLine("    txtstream.WriteLine(""%>"")")
        txtstream.WriteLine("    txtstream.WriteLine(""</table>"")")
        txtstream.WriteLine("    txtstream.WriteLine(""</body>"")")
        txtstream.WriteLine("    txtstream.WriteLine(""</html>"")")
        txtstream.Close()

    End Sub

    Private Sub End_The_XSL_Code()


        txtstream.WriteLine("    txtstream.WriteLine(""</table>"")")
        txtstream.WriteLine("    txtstream.WriteLine(""</body>"")")
        txtstream.WriteLine("    txtstream.WriteLine(""</html>"")")
        txtstream.WriteLine("    txtstream.WriteLine(""</xsl:template>"")")
        txtstream.WriteLine("    txtstream.WriteLine(""</xsl:stylesheet>"")")
        txtstream.WriteLine("    txtstream.Close()")
        txtstream.Close()

    End Sub

    Private Sub End_All_Others()

        txtstream.Close()

    End Sub


End Module
```